One Soul at a Time

Reclaiming the Christian Mission to Care for the Soul

By
Dale A. Wright

CONTENTS

Acknowledgments

I want to thank the staff at the Canyon View Vineyard Church in Grand Junction, Colorado who believed in the dream of a peer counseling team, gave me the classroom and cell phone and turned me loose. Your willingness to step out in faith from what is "normal church" into the unknown has been a blessing to many.

I owe a special thank you to my wife, Laurie, who not only can spell and diagram a sentence, but has kept me encouraged. Thank you for believing in this book project. Thank you also for listening to ideas and accepting the good ones while showing grace for the rest. I love you.

And finally I want to thank every peer counselor who has sat through the training classes and helped me sort through what information is helpful and what is not. Thank you for the "Yes, I can take that assignment," from the providers I have called throughout the years. You have been pioneers in a ministry that is reclaiming the work of the church. You are amazing and Spirit led. Special thanks to Pat Daub, Bob Litsheim, John Jessup, and Bob Clifford who are rock solid supports.

Preface

This book is written for everyone who desires greater authentic spiritual relationships. It is for those in mission work, ministry of all types, and for everyone who is seeking to plant the gospel seed and better connect with the soil where the seeds are planted. This information has been helpful to employers, co-workers, pastors, friends, husbands and wives, and parents. It is for all who are searching for ways to make those deeper connections that we all long for.

This book is also for those who wish to start sustainable peer counseling ministries in their churches. It is a difficult ministry, but God is already there working. It is just a matter of joining Him.

I use the term "peer counselor" to refer to those who do not have professional training and are working on a volunteer basis. "Mentoring" is a form of peer counseling that simply means counseling in less formal relationships and with more self disclosure on the counselors' part.

It has been suggested to use the words, "patrons," "seekers," "Soul Care receivers," or "counselees" to refer to people requesting peer counseling. But for this book, I chose "clients" to refer to anyone seeking our help.

All scriptures are quoted from the New International Version unless otherwise noted.

Like apples of gold in settings of silver
Is a word spoken in right circumstances.

Proverbs 25:11 (NASB)

Introduction

The story of Moses and the burning bush has always fascinated me. It is a great story with many applications. I've heard numerous sermons based on this story but none on the character to whom I relate the most: the bush. I find it interesting that God chose something as ordinary and unqualified as a bush to communicate His message to Moses.

The bush could not talk, had no outstanding spiritual qualities and, for all we know, could have been a thorn bush. But God used it. He used it to speak to His chosen leader. This bush was not a mighty Cedar of Lebanon or a majestic Oak. It was not qualified in any measure. Some might refer to it as a weed or bramble bush. Why did God use it? The answer is simple: God used the bush because it was available.

This bush stood in the middle of nowhere with no expectations or plans to make something big happen. But something big did happen: God happened. He came down and came into the bush. That bush experienced the presence of Almighty God, the Creator of our vast cosmos speaking through it. God set the bush afire. The bush's part was to be available. That was its only real quality. It was available when God needed it. God's presence made up for the lack of qualification and experience.

The lesson for me is clear: I can do nothing apart from my Creator. My talents are only useful when I am energized by God. It does not matter what the Creator has or has not given to me. What matters is that I bring these things to Him so He may use them.

There are times when God asks us to do things that seem way out of our league. It might be a scary and seemingly impossible undertaking. It might be something we have never done or even thought of doing. I have heard people who feel they are called by God to counsel the hurting but feel a lack of confidence for the task. They were scared, unsure and had serious doubts. Oddly enough, that is the best place to start: humble and dependent upon God alone. Helping others with their personal problems is never easy, but with God's involvement, it is powerful. If you have the talent and experience of a bush in the middle of nowhere, welcome to peer counseling.

Chapter 1
Why this Book is Needed

This book is part of a restoration movement to reclaim the right and responsibility of the Church to care for the soul. Somehow along the way we, as God's people, have veered off our divinely appointed mission. We have busied ourselves with many spiritual activities including preaching, teaching, praying, gathering into small groups etc. All of these are essential, but I fear we have forgotten one of the most important elements to which we are called. We have wandered off the path and lost our ability to care for hurting souls.

When the people around us are in trouble and need help with personal problems we so often wilt and send them away to someone else; someone downtown with a college degree. We are willing to hand our responsibility to professional counselors who may or may not hold Christian values, but we feel safe in doing so because they are licensed by the state. As a church, we also defer to "professional Christians;" our clergy who are often too busy for ongoing counseling or have never received adequate training for the task.

The community around us has followed this reasoning and does not consider the Church as a place to receive emotional and psychological help. I have found that the word "counseling" is now more closely associated with secular psychologists than with the clergy and Christianity. This has not always been the case.

Christians are often perceived as judgmental and lacking in real world wisdom. In the eyes of the world, Christians have become irrelevant in addressing personal and psychological problems. We have participated in this shift toward irrelevance by freely outsourcing our divinely appointed work. We have bought the lie that we are less qualified to provide counseling than are the professional psychologists. By setting down our tools we have lost our skills and have deferred our work of caring for the soul exclusively to our Christian leaders and to "expert" non-believers. Scripture makes it abundantly clear that God desires for us to care for one another's souls and has given us the tools to do so. But as the church stands now, we have wandered away from our divinely appointed mission.

What I Heard When I Was Not Listening

The telling of my story will enable you to understand the perspective from which this book is written. I see myself as very ordinary and common. This is important to remember because I think most of God's work is done by people who do not stand out for their extraordinary abilities. His power is seen through our weakness (I Corinthians1:26-31). In my case, the weakness is a vast and open field.

It was during high school that I became a Christian and began my personal relationship with the Creator of the universe. I commenced my lifetime study of scripture and began to slowly absorb the supernatural wisdom found in the pages of the Bible. At the same time, I was fascinated with the field of psychology so I headed off to college to study it. I was intrigued by those very smart-looking bearded men smoking pipes while scribbling ideas on their note pads. What is it they know? How do they help people? What is the great wisdom they possess? I set out to become one of those great wise men; one of those men who people gladly pay to talk with and who were held in such high regard. I could not wait to learn the mysterious wisdom of the Psychologists.

While in graduate school, I listened to hundreds of lectures, read piles of books, spent untold hours in the library reading research articles and subjected myself to numerous workshops and seminars. I was on a quest for that great psychological wisdom. While most of the information that I learned was interesting, some of it was particularly intriguing. In one of my beginning counseling psychology classes, the professor discussed character qualities that would predict the making of a good counselor. Much research and discussion went into this foundational topic, for it is central in a good counseling relationship. What is it about a counselor that makes him or her "good" at counseling? Personality characteristics were considered, and it was concluded that regardless of the theoretical orientation of the counselor, these qualities were necessary to be effective as a helping professional: warm, genuine, concrete, showing empathy, and giving their clients something called "unconditional positive regard."[1]

This was cutting edge information at the time but it sounded strangely familiar to me. It very accurately described the character qualities of Jesus Christ. This ancient truth had been rediscovered! When you display God's character to another person, it is therapeutic. It is life changing. The fruit of the spirit in Galatians chapter 5 describes the qualities found in this study and adds a few more as well. Here was one of the great nuggets of truth for which I had been searching, but it was borrowed from the people of God who had known of it for thousands of years. This was fascinating but not exactly what I thought I was looking for.

Another study compared the counseling ability of trained professional counselors with ordinary people like home-makers, plumbers, store clerks, etc. They trained the peer counselors and provided supervision then sent them off to do counseling. Their results were compared to the results of trained professional therapists. The researchers found that the non-professional counselors were equally effective in helping people.[2] In fact, they had better results with some population groups than did the professional counselors! At the time, this study was disturbing since I was spending so much time and money to become a professional counselor.

I also was unhappy to learn that psychologists had significantly higher divorce rates and higher suicide rates than the general population.[3] Counselors should be the most well adjusted, satisfied, balanced people of all. Therapists taught others how to live. They coached people on marriage, parenting and grief, and they helped others discover the meaning of life. Why weren't they discovering and embracing this for themselves? In addition, I discovered that psychologists are less religious than those in other professions.[4] This was odd. The very people who guide others through life had not connected with the Author of Life. This disconnection from God, the higher incidence of suicide and divorce, and the fact that others were able to perform counseling equally as well was puzzling and troubling.

There was another remarkable moment I remember from Graduate school. We were studying psychopathology (the study of mental illness) in one of our final classes before graduation. For three years we had been intently examining subjects like neurological psychology, personality theory, psychometric testing, clinical psychology, family therapy, counseling psychology, statistics in psychology and many others. We were almost ready to be placed into the work force as "therapists" but we were feeling a little insecure and unprepared for the daunting task of healing the broken world. One student raised his hand and asked a question. "What are the interventions we are to use to change people?" The professor gave an answer, but we were not satisfied with it. Someone else asked a similar follow-up question. Again an answer was given, but we were still dissatisfied. The questioning continued until we finally gave up and moved to another topic.

We felt insecure with the knowledge we had. We knew we were lacking something in our education and training, but did not know what it was. We did not know how to express the question and the professor was not helpful in answering it. It was a strange interaction that stuck in my mind. We were still left with a feeling that something was absent; a key piece of the puzzle was missing. Looking back, I realize what I was searching for. I wanted to know, "How do people change?" I had learned a great deal of information and had started counseling others, but I still did not comprehend how people change. I was able to witness change in my clients, but did not understand why it happened in some but not in others. Some individuals seem to have resiliency and power to make changes while others could make changes for short periods and later seemed to sink further into their problems. To make it more confusing, I noticed that factors such as dysfunctional family histories, child abuse, past substance abuse, etc. did not necessarily have negative impacts as I predicted they should. Some people had the odds stacked against them but managed to change anyway, while others struggled to change even though their histories were relatively healthy.

I believed the culturally taught notion that psychologists alone held the wisdom to care for people's souls. After jumping into the middle of it, I realized their wisdom was incomplete and much of what they possessed was borrowed from Christian sources. It was very troubling to know that those in the profession had an abnormally high frequency of problems themselves. While the whole experience of graduate school was beneficial for me, in my opinion, huge pieces of the puzzle were missing in this profession. Sadly, this missing information was not noticed by the professionals themselves.

The Apostle Paul writes in Romans 1:16-17:

> "I am not ashamed of the gospel, because it is the power of God for the salvation of everyone who believes: first for the Jew, then for the Gentile. For in the gospel a righteousness from God is revealed, a righteousness that is by faith from first to last, just as it is written: 'The righteous will live by faith.'"

Salvation is in the power of the gospel. Not only eternal salvation from our sin, but also salvation from the bondages of every sort of problem we may experience in this life. This is one of the missing pieces that a Christian counselor possesses and most psychologists don't. God gave us a complete set of tools to care for each other. The odds of success against a problem are not predicted by your family history, past child abuse, socioeconomic status, or whether your mama loved you. It is in God's power for you to change.

We need revival in the heart of the saved. With heavenly wisdom and care, we must step out in faith and believe that we are the chosen ones to help people through difficulties in life. We have the help of the Mighty Counselor who loves us unconditionally. He created us. He knows exactly how to help in times of trouble, and when we have veered off course. To help us even further, our Heavenly Father reached down and inspired the scriptures so we can read His instructions clearly.

We have a calling to do the work. We have His Great Spirit to lead us. We have His written words to read. Yes, we are a well-equipped army lying fast asleep in the battle field. Do we have the courage to rise?

This book is written for those who wish to rise and reclaim the mission to counsel others who are hurting. If you have an unquenchable burning in your soul to become what God has made you to be then keep reading and searching. I have witnessed that everyday-Christians are gifted to do extraordinary things. They have humility and gentleness and an undying supernatural love for others. God uses these qualities to divinely inspire peer counselors. Many have doubts and insecurities, but in willing hearts God's Spirit conquers these obstacles.

The information in this book is born out of experience. In January, 2004, The Canyon View Vineyard Church in Grand Junction, Colorado started a ministry called Soul Care. God blessed this ministry with a core group of volunteers who committed themselves to bring the ministry to maturity. We started with a vision that God's Holy Spirit could use ordinary Christians to provide Biblical counsel to others. Because I am a licensed professional counselor, I provided training and supervision. We prayed hard, rolled up our sleeves, called forth all the courage we could muster and sat down to listen intently to the hurting, confused, and enslaved. Miracles happened. Healing for the soul was realized. Those who were hurting were comforted, the confused found direction and purpose, and many others found freedom and restoration in Jesus. It was difficult, but it was "fun" and tremendously rewarding. Since many of our requests for help come from married couples, we developed a marriage mentoring ministry. God has blessed this work and blessed each of us. Peer counseling ministries have spread into other congregations in the area. It is obvious that His will is to help the hurting, and we are privileged and amazed at how He has used us to answer prayers. Not every story we hear has a happy ending. At times, we see no progress. We have witnessed things worsen, but we still feel satisfied that we are there offering hope, encouragement and ultimate victory through Jesus Christ. We persevered and God provided us with the energy.

We have found strength by staying close together. This is a critical part of the equation for long term success. Peer counseling and mentoring are difficult, and it is only by sharing encouragement and wisdom that we continue to go forward. You will read in later chapters about our carefully organized support system for individual peer counselors and marriage mentors. We are a body and each of us has different experiences from which to draw and have been gifted to work in different ways. Peer counseling is most successful when we work *together* under God's authority and guidance. Although this organizational support may not be possible in all cases, it is important that you offer yourself as a helper with support or oversight from others. The work of counseling can be emotionally difficult and complicated, so others around you will help ensure that you do not get burned out or become immersed in the problems of those who are seeking your help.

Please note that some situations do require the attention of professional counselors, especially in times of crisis. Some people are extremely taxing due to personality issues, and/or difficulties related to mental illness and medications. It is necessary to seek professional counselors in situations that involve domestic violence, pervasive substance abuse or suicidal and homicidal thoughts. Legal requirements for reporting child abuse and homicidal threats need to be handled by professionals as well. It is an added blessing when these professional counselors are Christians, but it is not always possible.

Chapter 2
The Battlefield for the Soul

Before Christians can reclaim our role as those who care for souls, we must understand the forces that surround us and shape our thinking and behavior. The cultural context in which we exist has a great effect on the way we behave as human beings. Our spiritual behaviors of serving, praying and even understanding scriptures are partially fashioned by the context of our culture.

As you well know, the world's influence is not always positive. In John 17, Jesus describes his disciples as remaining in the world, but not being of the world. The message is understood and applied with a wide range of religious practices. I observe some Christians who have separated themselves from the world's influences to the point they are not effectively able to influence unbelievers at all. They are too detached, isolated and unnecessarily "weird" to others around them. On the other extreme, others have lived in the world to the degree their influence is negligible because their values and behavior are undifferentiated from the nonbeliever's.

I do not believe we are to be completely isolated from the influences of the world. If we are "in the world," we will be woven within its fabric; influenced by it, but not in a way that draws us away from Him. He wants us to be part of our communities and thus living in the context of our time, but not participating in the activities that harm us spiritually. The Apostle Paul writes in Romans 12:2 that you should not "conform any longer to the pattern of this world, but be transformed by the renewing of your mind." Jesus spoke and interacted with people in the context of the Jewish culture of his time. He challenged many of their cultural and religious practices, but did so as a Jewish man in the day and time that he chose to reveal Himself. This cultural dance with the world of the nonbeliever is one that we need to continually evaluate. We must ensure that we are at just the right distance from the world that we have an impact on it, but not so close that we are not able to conform ourselves to the likeness of Jesus.

This chapter includes my observations of how the culture of modern psychology (the world) has influenced Christians. Both the field of psychology and the Bible hold truths about counseling, many of which are identical. The term "psychology" literally means "the word of psyche," translated to mean "the understanding of the mind." So psychology, in a general sense, has existed since the beginning of time. The Bible and other books have contained knowledge about this topic for thousands of years. Psychology was organized as a field of scientific study approximately one hundred years ago. Since that time it has exploded in popularity and continues to grow in its knowledge of the "psyche." Currently, there are many widely attended schools of psychology where people can study this growing body of understanding about the" psyche" and become professional Psychologists.

As with any area of study, where one begins has a lot to do with where one ends up. The field of psychology began with men who did not value the wisdom found in the Bible. In my opinion, they did not start from a solid foundation so, through the years, the field of knowledge grew separate from God's explanations of the "psyche."

Even though the disciplined study of psychology has only existed for a short time, it has grown incredibly powerful in our world. Unfortunately, I see that we have uncritically accepted many ideas from modern psychology that are contrary to a Godly world view. We have not kept a proper distance from the things that can harm us. Even though I hold a graduate degree in psychology, I do not blindly defend it. Neither do I dismiss its usefulness. But I am, above all else, a Christian. If there is a contradiction between the teaching of psychology and the teaching of God, God always wins the debate, even if I do not understand the reasoning behind His ways. This book is written from a Christian world view.

Psychology has profoundly impacted our culture and the church. Because of its humanistic roots, we need to be especially vigilant when examining its influence on us. I do not intend to leave the impression that psychology should be totally avoided. It is especially helpful to Christians when it is used as a tool for observation. Insights can be achieved from this profession that would not be noticed through a Christian unobjective point of view.

The following sections highlight why I believe modern psychology is pulling us away from foundational truths which are given by God Himself.

Psychology and Christianity

To discuss peer counseling and mentoring we must dabble into the messy topic of how Christianity and science relate to each other. Whether you have consciously thought through this topic or not, you have made conclusions about it. Your conclusions will drastically impact your ability to counsel or mentor others so let's take a look at this together.

The scientific study of human behavior, commonly known as psychology, is growing ever more powerful in our culture and is encroaching into the territory of caring for the soul. It is my observation that when most people think of counseling they do not first think of counseling in a church, they think of professional counselors like psychologists. This shift in perception and psychology's advancement into the territory of caring for the soul are of great concern to me.

Psychology begins by building a belief system based on truth gained from the scientific method and interpretation of data. Theology begins by finding its truth from revelation and interpretation of scripture. This difference in beginnings creates a relationship between the two that can be both complimentary and antagonistic. It is commonly believed that the field of psychology and Christianity are "separate but equal." That is, they do not often interact directly and their different understandings compliment each other without conflict. This notion sees the soul cared for in the spiritual realm of the church, and the psyche cared for in the realm of psychology, without overlap. This view is simplistic and does not take into account the directives of scripture that involve every aspect of life from the cradle to the grave.

There would be no shared territory if psychology would stay within the arena of observation and description only, but it often does not. It makes value judgments regarding which behaviors should and should not be accepted. It has its own versions of right and wrong, functional and dysfunctional, normal and abnormal, acceptable and pathological. Although the word "sin" is never used in the psychological disciplines, it clearly defines what sin is to them.

There are many sub-fields of psychology, such as social psychology, industrial psychology, experimental psychology and many others, but counseling psychology is the field in which differences in the definition of sin show their ugly heads the most. Christianity and psychology are not separate-but-equal. They fiercely compete in the same arena of ideas, especially in the counseling office. The value system in the field of counseling psychology differs from that of Christians who accept the Bible as a standard for defining sin. These differing systems of morality create fierce territorial battles that leave both sides disinterested in learning from the other. There are a few individuals who ambitiously try to embrace both psychology and Christian counseling, but with so many opportunities for incongruity, individuals will gravitate toward one side or the other.

I believe psychology is helpful but not essential. Therefore, my approach is to first completely embrace God and all that He teaches, then take what is helpful, but not contradictory, from psychology. Consider a claim made in ancient scripture:

> "Grace and peace be multiplied to you in the knowledge of God and of Jesus our Lord; seeing that His divine power has granted to us everything pertaining to life and godliness, through the true knowledge of Him who called us by His own glory and excellence" (2nd Peter 1:2-3).

This verse has an outrageous claim. Did you hear it? God has "given us everything pertaining to life and godliness." As a graduate student studying psychology, I was having a conversation with a conservative preacher. He read this verse to me and basically explained that God gave us everything we need for psychological health and therefore, Christians did not need to study psychology. This, of course, got me excited and the debate was on. As I labored to persuade him that we needed to study psychology, he countered my points with scriptures.

Finally, out of frustration, I informed him that he was being closed minded, which I thought was a pretty clever way out of losing a debate. He countered with the statement that, "God is closed minded. He knows everything already so He does not need to learn from you. We cannot tell God anything He does not know. Why look elsewhere when the Creator of the universe, who is all knowing, has said he gave us everything we need? The source is absolutely perfect and the information is absolutely complete."

At the time, I did not appreciate how important this conversation would become for me. As time passes and as I log in more experience in life and observe the lives of others, I am more convinced this is absolutely true. God *has* given us all we need for life. Today, if I had to choose between my knowledge from graduate school or the Sermon on the Mount, I would choose the Sermon on the Mount (Matthew chapters 5, 6 & 7). There is more wisdom in those few pages of the Bible than in the tall stack of books and articles I have read on psychology. I am not suggesting that the body of knowledge called psychology is without value. I want to simply state that there is great depth of wisdom to be found in the scriptures, and this wisdom is more than sufficient to be an excellent peer counselor. And not only is there a wealth of wisdom in the scriptures, but God's Spirit is very interested in helping us understand and use it. This is a huge bonus that psychology cannot claim. As Christians, we have a Guiding Spirit to teach and instruct us.

In our modern culture we drive cars and our culture is ever evolving around our ability to be mobile. Cars are helpful, but are they essential for life? Because our societies have evolved around cars and our ability to use them, it would be more difficult not to have one. But we can still meet our basic needs and never own a car. Other cultures have not built their societies around the automobile and are fully able to live happily without them. Therefore, we can conclude that cars are helpful to human beings, but not essential. Likewise, psychology can assist Christians in their lives, but it is not essential. Many people are completely unaware of the existence of the field of psychology and yet live in contentment.

The practical application for peer counseling is this: You do not need a degree in psychology to truly help someone. This whole chapter is written so that you can have confidence in this fact. You may be challenged from every direction, but be assured - the Author of Life has given us all we need. Many may not believe this at first, including those you are helping, community professionals, and even church leaders. (Critics can come from everywhere, even unlikely sources.) But the truth is a very difficult thing to suppress, and honest critics will see that the scriptures contain complete knowledge for the training of peer counselors.

In the last chapter you will find case studies of Soul Care providers and testimonies from church leaders who have experienced first hand the benefits of peer counseling ministries. You will read testimonies of God using ordinary individuals to change lives, yet they do not have degrees in counseling. Some people initially have strong reservations about sharing their issues with peer counselors who do not have professional psychology degrees, but after beginning the supernatural relationships with peer counselors who truly care for their souls, these doubts vanish.

Do not feel obligated to defend Christian peer counseling. If the opportunity arises and you feel equipped to do so, then make a defense. But for most, it is not necessary. Your quiet and gentle spirit will speak for you. What matters most are the people who come to you for help. Your relationship will be all they need to experience the value in it.

As I was finishing undergraduate studies, I asked a professor which graduate school I should attend so that I would be perceived as a good counselor. His reply surprised me. He told me that most people do not really care what school you attended or even what degree you have, they care if you can help them. So please resist the cultural notion that counseling falls in the domain of psychologists, because it simply does not. Psychologists are late-comers into the field; it is Christians who have the tools for caring for the souls of people, and have done so for thousands of years.

"Some trust in chariots and some trust in horses, but we trust in the name of the Lord our God" (Psalm 20:7).

The Myth of Neutral Position

To the best of my ability, this book is based on Biblical principles. We live in a time where religious neutrality is in fashion. Science and most forms of media strive to be unbiased and religiously neutral, but I propose that this is completely impossible. We think and communicate through our own value systems. If we attempt to be neutral by hiding our values, our nonverbal behavior, even if ever so slight, will convey our position. Allegedly, psychologists are especially practiced and educated to not show their biases and values. It is considered unprofessional to promote one's own values while counseling others. Carl Rogers, the founder of humanistic psychology, taught non-directive therapy practices such as reflecting back to clients only what they said or expressed previously. He thought that in doing this he was not directing the client but, in fact, he was. The tone of his voice, the expression of his face when they were talking, and exactly what he chose to reflect back were all showing his values and directing his clients.

During my years in graduate school, I believed this "neutral position" idea and strove to practice it in my own sessions. But, to be honest, I always failed. I failed because it is impossible to be neutral. Even hard core atheists have a foundation of values that spells what is right and wrong to them. They have "sins" that are not acceptable to them and their behavior transmits these values to others, even if they try to conceal them.

Human beings were not created to be religiously neutral. In fact, Jesus taught that "you are either for me or against me,"

(Matthew 12:30). There is no need to search for shades of gray in that statement. When I begin my counseling appointments I inform people that I intend to help them have closer relationships with God and hope that they live with Him in eternity. I still listen very intently and stay on subjects that interest them but, ultimately, I direct them as gently and lovingly as possible to change in ways I think will help them relate to God in a deeper and more meaningful way; no apologies, no pretenses of neutrality. God is not neutral and he does not want us to be neutral about Him when we are reaching out to others.

In the church we cannot allow ourselves to become passive and adopt a position of neutrality. We have become a culture that highly values tolerance and non-offensiveness. These values are held to be more important than searching for and finding truth. Jesus never taught tolerance. In love, he taught about sin, repentance and forgiveness. He taught an unchangeable moral standard that was very offensive to some people. The problem with tolerance is that there is always another level of depravity waiting in line to be accepted. The line between good and bad always moves toward more depravity. In this tolerant system of morality, the only "sin" is non-acceptance.

When we are counseling and mentoring, sin must not be accepted. With love and grace, we must take a firm position against it. This is not an easy skill to learn and most beginning counselors struggle with it. In later chapters I have more to say about correcting sin without scaring people away or causing them to feel judged.

As Christian peer counselors and mentors, we have great strength. We do not pretend to be neutral, but rather have a mission to hold to a God-given standard. We cannot apologize for holding Christian beliefs and morals as our foundation.

Our values and morals are gifts from God and are sources of strength and guidance. We must stand firm, without apology, as *Christian* peer counselors.

The Flaw of Measured Outcomes

Scientists want to measure everything they can. That is how they know something is real - if it can be quantified and measured in some way. In the scientific study of psychology, scientists measure whether counselors are effective in their treatment. It is beneficial to determine if a counseling intervention is working so that we know whether we are using our time wisely. We want to improve our methods whenever possible so that we can achieve greater success. But this is the exact point where science, psychology and Christianity part ways. As Christians, the greatest outcome of our lives is to be with God after we die and to help as many people as possible to do the same. God does not allow us to see heaven, so science cannot study our ultimate successful outcome.

This is where the problem begins. In fact, in the process of pursuing our greatest goals, we may appear maladjusted. Jesus Himself was described as a man of suffering (Isaiah 53:3) as He fulfilled His mission on earth. When we seek to imitate Him and find our meaning and purpose, we are not aligned with typical measurable outcomes. Our greatest goal is citizenship in heaven, so our interest in seeking pleasure and happiness in this world is not as critical. The idea of measuring outcomes is a noble one, except that the greatest human outcome is not measurable and the process of achieving this goal could appear counterproductive as observed by unbelievers.

As Christian counselors and mentors, we look to scripture to determine success. We can help people pursue the eternal purposes that God has planned for their lives. This outcome may not look as successful psychologically to the outside observer. In fact, I have noticed that God brings discipline and/or difficulties to life to refine character or to bring about needed insight and change. If we work to take away this "trouble" in someone's life, we may be inadvertently working against God's plans. Naturally, we want to see a difference in the way the people feel, but that may not be the best course for them. God may use consequences of bad behavior to bring people to a place where they are better able to change. Our job is not necessarily to help people "feel better," it is to help them "be better." Always consider the bigger picture and the greater good of a person, not just what the world or a psychologist wants to see or measure.

Since science cannot measure our desired outcomes, we still need to ask ourselves the question, "Do counseling and mentoring really work?" A better question might be, "While receiving counseling and mentoring, do people develop closer relationships with God?" Based on my observations of their lives, they most certainly do. As a ministry leader, I witness people increase their desire to seek God and live according to His wishes. I see the fruit of the spirit (Galatians 5) manifest itself to a greater degree in a life after seeking help from a Christian peer counselor. These are indicators that peer counseling works.

I find the best definition of success in Psalm 23:6, "Surely love and gentleness will follow me all the days of my life and I will dwell in the house of the Lord forever." This is my goal: to live a life filled with love and to live with my gracious and merciful Creator for eternity. What else is there? Deep inside, I think this is what we all desire. Even the most committed atheist is unwittingly searching for this. He may be lost and completely on the wrong track, but he still has this yearning buried inside. The desire to seek and relate to God can be ignored and covered up by other desires but, I believe, never goes away. Add this to the list of great gifts we receive from

God: An undying longing to be with Him! Our job as counselors and mentors is to help others find this too.

The Myth that Man is Inherently Good

The idea that man is inherently good gives us warm feelings. A foundational tenant of humanistic psychology is that man is good, and if he is released from his inhibitions and hang-ups he will behave in a loving way to all. Good humanists believe that mankind fight and kill one another only because of problems created in our psyche from the past. They believe if a person is raised in a loving environment that is rich in opportunities, he or she will be good because that is his/her basic nature. As much as I want to believe this, I cannot agree. The Bible says in Ephesians 2:3 that "we are by nature children of wrath," (NASB) and our hearts are continually set on evil. Written in Psalm 14 and again many years later in Romans 3:9-18, God tells us that "none are good, not even one." These verses might, at first, seem to exaggerate this truth. After all, there are individuals who commit their lives to helping others with complete disregard for their own needs. Even people who are completely unreligious seem to have interest in doing good and helping others. Some of the nicest people I have met are not Christians, but have outdone Christians in their kindness and good works.

Most of us seem to be virtuous people regardless of our background and religious orientation. But if you look a little closer, our goodness is not that good. From the beginning of our lives, as young children, we are selfish and unconcerned about others around us. We cry, kick and scream if we do not get our way. Slowly, over time, this nature is trained out of us to some degree. But when all inhibition is removed, we show our true nature again. For example, when working in a local detention facility performing mental health evaluations, it was my assignment to talk with people who had just been arrested.

Many of these people were average citizens who had consumed alcohol to the point of intoxication. In this state of inhibition, they committed horrendous acts such as domestic violence, murder and child sexual abuse. They would have never dreamed of doing these things normally and are quite shocked at their own behavior once they recover from their binge. The alcohol removed their inhibitions and revealed the sinful nature.

I have heard many secular counselors advise clients to do whatever they want to do; whatever makes them happy and fulfilled. This ever growing, popular idea of doing what feels good is a dangerous trap that has led to many broken marriages and families. God's Holy Spirit and His written word are strong sources of illumination and control in this area. Because of our sinful nature we need God's help to control ourselves. We also need help from our Christian brothers and sisters. To think and behave otherwise has proved disastrous in our culture as well as in our personal lives. As counselors and mentors we need to stand firm in the truth by encouraging self-control and restraint from our sinful nature.

As Christian peer counselors, we can understand the core nature of those to whom we listen. This is an immense tactical strength for us. New age or humanistic counselors are at a disadvantage because they are working to let out the "good person" deep inside which is not there. Christian counselors work to overcome the core nature within each person by bringing the nature of God into the core of each individual. Because we start in the right place by understanding the true nature of the person, we have a much greater chance to help that person out of his present darkness and trouble.

When Psychology and Science Become Religion

As individuals and as mankind, we are left with a great many unknowns. Science and personal observations leave us short of understanding our world. We are surrounded by mysteries that are well beyond our ability to observe if we are brave enough to admit it. So we have to fill in these intellectual voids with information from sources other than human observations.

Science is objective, scientists are not. Here originates a great problem: scientists often fall into the trap of going beyond what science has revealed to them. They make conclusions outside of their data. They may believe they are being objective, but are projecting their personal beliefs into the data. For instance, many scientists observe our world and the universe but do not see or observe an intelligent Creator. They mistakenly conclude that there is no God, rather than concluding that they do not see God, or that they simply do not know.

Atheistic scientists may mistakenly believe that their conclusions about God come from science when, in fact, their conclusions are derived from other sources. Some scientists put science and psychology into the place where God truly belongs. The limits of science are essentially ignored and faith in God is viewed as foolishness because God cannot be seen. These scientific zealots see religion as the "old science" that has been deemed obsolete or no longer adequate to care for the soul.

Others, like Christian psychologists, accept that truth can come from more than one source, and can fully embrace God and His revelation to man. They can also accept information that has come by way of the scientific method. The scientific method can be a tool to help us learn more about ourselves. It can be applied along with wisdom and God-revealed truths. Higher education and the intensive study of any subject, with proper perspective, can be a blessing and a tool for mankind and for the church. But when it is put in the place of God and thus made into an idol, then it becomes problematic and often antagonistic toward Christians.

I say all of this to warn that "counseling professionals" may look down on you because you are operating from a Christian world view. Some may see Christian peer counselors as "unscientific" in our approach, and this is unapologetically true. We do not claim to base our approach on the study of science. We may use science where it is helpful, but much of our approach to helping others comes from scripture and from our great Holy Spirit.

The truth is that science is miserably lacking in real information on how to care for the soul of man. Of course, this view is not shared by most secular psychologists. They believe their conclusions are based on science and empirical data, but it is their religion, not their science, upon which they are basing many of their conclusions.

This is one of our strengths. We know the source of our beliefs and do not pretend otherwise. We are upfront and genuine about our source of knowledge of the soul and where we get our instruction to care for it. It is revealed by God through His scriptures and His Spirit.

The Power is in the Gospel, not Human Insight and Ambition

Most models of counseling are insight driven. They strive to give the client more knowledge about themselves, thus creating better opportunity to change. These "figure it out models" are popular for therapists and clients alike. These models put the professionals in the expert's seat because they have the education and the knowledge. They use specialized vocabulary to describe various human conditions. The client is placed into a subordinate and sometimes passive position of receiving information about themselves from the counselor. Unfortunately, "getting new insights into self" and "changing self" are not necessarily linked together. Knowing that you are an alcoholic and having insights about what created this behavior do not mean that you can stop drinking. Knowing why you do something does not give you the ability to stop. In fact, seeking "self insight" can become an addiction in itself and a distraction from changing.

This "figure it out model" is so pervasive in our culture that it has become the goal of many Christians and the intent of many sermons to gain more insight into the "self." We are encouraged to use this insight to change through human effort. Although insight may seemingly cause change, the change is only temporary. Therefore more information about the "self" is needed and the addiction cycle is born.

I think a better model for change is the "model of surrender." This model is all about giving up control and interest in self insight. Instead, the focus is on Jesus and His purpose for you. Self confidence is traded for "Godfidence." We rely on God's abilities rather than our own, and on His confidence in us. We rely on God's understanding rather than our own. This is a foreign concept to most people and even for many Christians. We hear the words "surrender to God," but seek the "self" instead.

The implications for peer counselors are great. Do not fall into the trap of being "the expert" by dispensing advice and information. It will not likely lead to permanent change and could easily foster dependency upon you instead of God. This is not what people truly need. They are coming to you for help, but are most likely seeking self insight and want you to help them find it. The current may be flowing the other way, but they need to keep the focus on their relationship with God and help develop their ability to listen to Him and accept His direction.

It is truly a paradox: surrender self to find peace and purpose for self. There are many verses in scripture that teach of this paradox. Romans chapter 6 is a personal favorite that beautifully states that we have died to our sin and to ourselves and by God's grace we are fully alive and free.

It is abundantly clear from scripture that God desires for us to counsel others. There are many external forces from our environment and culture that are working against us as we attempt to accomplish our mission. Science may encroach into our space and criticize our outcomes because they cannot measure them. They may see the source of our knowledge as old and incomplete, and falsely believe that mankind just needs better circumstances to be better behaved. Let them believe what they may, but stand firm in your effort to show God and His eternal Kingdom to hurting people. We can accept psychological teachings when they are, in fact, helpful and do not contradict scripture, but be assured that we have a complete guide for counseling and are the ones for the job.

Chapter 3
The Danger From Within

Our western culture has a strong influence on our thinking. I am not a philosopher or a theologian, but I do want to share a few observations about tendencies in modern Christianity that are negatively impacting ministry within the church. These next few points demand our attention. If we look the other way, they will continue to grow and harm the work in God's Kingdom. We need to take a look at ourselves, the good and the bad, so we may know who we are and what is around us. Only then will we have a solid place from which to start.

Where Has All the Sin Gone?

We have almost successfully eliminated the notion of sin in our culture. I have noticed that people react to the word "sin" like it is on top of the politically incorrect word list. This short little word is at the heart of the battle of absolute moral standards. The existence of sin shows there is right and wrong, that there are fixed and unchanging standards to follow and also consequences for breaking the standards. No person naturally likes to admit wrong behavior, and it is growing more acceptable to think of good and bad behavior as being relative to the situation rather than hard and fixed.

The world has intimidated the church to the point that we rarely hear the word "sin" in a sermon, much less, admonishment to deal with it. We call it "dysfunction," "abnormality," "making wrong choices," etc; terms designed to make it palatable to our egos and supposedly harmless to our souls. But in truth, sin carries more harm than anything else in existence. It is poison to the psyche and the soul. Sin wreaks havoc with the relationship between our spirit and mind, between ourselves and our loved ones, and most importantly, between ourselves and God. Our creator sees sin as serious enough to send His Son to die. Our viewpoint should mirror His.

"Those whom I love, I reprove and chasten; so be zealous and repent" (Revelation 3:19).

Once you recognize the sin as sin and repent, then it no longer has mastery over you.

This tendency to deny sin will be seen in people as they enter into counseling relationships. We can bring them closer to true mental health and freedom by refusing to participate in the cultural notion that right and wrong are matters of human opinion.

We Are Losing Presence

Recently while on Facebook, I was looking for friends and had a bizarre thought: "Is God on Facebook?" I actually looked, and sure enough, there He was; God Almighty. The Lord Himself. I was stunned, but finally got the courage to send him a friend request. He never answered. How disappointing. You may have better luck. It turns out there are thousands of "Gods," "Jehovahs," and "God Almightys" on Facebook.

E-mail, Facebook, texting, cell phones, internet meetings and the next great innovation to advance our communication all lack the most important element of human communication: Human presence. We were created to interact face-to-face, toe-to-toe, cheek-to-cheek. To be in the same space, share the same air; there is no replacement. We do not understand this as a culture, and are headed into perilous waters with consequences greater than we may know. We are even moving away from physically holding our children. I often see babies not in their mothers' arms, but in plastic carriers. Babies can only see 18" in front of them, so we put them out of their range of sight; out of our presence.

All these things may seem small, but I'm not so sure they are. We are divinely created to relate to each other and to relate to Him. So many people struggle in their lives and do not make the connection that they suffer from loneliness. They are missing true human contact and contact with their loving Father. Take time to examine the way you connect with others. Is it superficial? Do you look people in the eye? Are you genuine and honest? How long do you listen before you begin thinking about yourself or thinking about your next response?

The current generation of families does not eat together as often as others have in the past. We watch TV and work on computers in separate rooms. I can mention many modern trends, such as daycare and longer work hours which take us away from true relationships with one another. This is why I believe so many people are flocking into counseling. We desire to be in the presence of someone who cares, or at least will care if he is paid. Applying this principle to peer counseling is straightforward. People are starving for real human connections and a true authentic relationship with God and fellow human beings, even though they most likely will not be able to recognize this.

I believe that as we increasingly disconnect in our society, psychological disorders will increase accordingly. This is especially seen in children who have been disconnected from the presence of their parents. As I continue to log in more hours as a counselor I see the devastation from broken families. In many cases, there has been physical, emotional, and sexual abuse, but the greater damage may be the separation of family members after these events. Many children have expressed to me their great sadness of not seeing a parent, and this seems to impact them more than the abusive incident. This is not true in every case, especially in cases of severe abuse, but as a society we are numb and dim-sighted when it comes to seeing the value of parental presence. Dr. Scott Simpson says it well:

> Love is being Present for the other before it is anything else—ahead of giving advice, or teaching, or sending gifts or money or anything else that might just as well be done 'from a distance.' This is why the Prodigal Son story is so beautiful (Luke 15:11-32). Even though the son doesn't appreciate his father's presence and only wants what he can get from him, once the son has gone far away, it's clear that the father's heart is STILL present for the son. The father is aware the moment the son approaches home, and runs out to close the gap between them— to put him in a robe, put a ring on his finger, kill the fatted calf and have a party! The father makes it clear WHY he is rejoicing; it's not because the son has paid him back, or even because the son will never make that mistake again. The father says, "This son of mine was dead, but has come back to life; he was lost, but now is found!" It's the being together that matters to the father. When we experience God's loving presence in that way, we then overflow with Present Love for others. Yes, we may give advice, instruction, suggestions, even hold

others accountable, but all of that will be bathed in full-on, relational love BECAUSE we are also very present for them. We are there—WITH them in the messes. That's God's incarnated definition of Love: "Emmanuel," God with us.[1]

Our Western Culture has Become Specialized and Busy.

There is more to life than merely increasing its speed.

Gandhi

When we look back just one hundred years, to a time with less technology, we see people who had a grasp of their surroundings. One individual could understand transportation, communication, and could produce his own food on the family farm. Life was difficult, but he could fix the wagon, send the telegram, and grow the tomatoes without hiring a specialist. Today, we take the car to the mechanic who has training in computer science. I do not know how many hours of my life have been spent reading manuals so that I am able to only partially understand how to use my phone. Most of us have no clue where our food comes from or how it gets to us. We are specialized. We each have our little part to do and everything else is done by someone else. This is not necessarily good or bad, it is just the way it is. I mention this because we have carried this trend toward specialization to the work of the church in areas where perhaps we should not have done so. When someone needs food we refer him to the food pantry. When someone needs prayer we send him to the prayer room. When someone has a dispute, we advise him to consult an attorney. Couples are sent to the pastor or to marriage counselors downtown with their marital problems. We have learned to take care of others by sending them to someone else. Is this what God desires us to do?

Part of this trend toward specialization is our tendency to refer counseling exclusively to the pastors/ministers. In most settings, the clergy spend much of their time counseling a few individuals, which allows less time to lead and pastor the flock. Counseling is part of the pastors' work, but it easily overtakes the rest of their responsibilities. And the fact that they are in pastoral positions does not mean they necessarily have the gift or desire to do the work of a counselor. When a church body has members who can share the responsibility of counseling, the pastors/ministers are freed up to perform other duties.

Another trend that influences our culture is the quick pace of life. Due to faster transportation and instant communication we can move ourselves and our things faster than ever before. We don't have to wait for our food, for our information, or for anything else nearly as long as in past generations. We want what we want, we get it, and we get it fast. This greater access to and availability of material goods and information keeps us seeking and consuming at a faster pace. Any free time is quickly taken up by something else that we think we cannot live without. It's like the classic film footage of Lucille Ball working in the chocolate factory; the conveyor belt just keeps moving faster and faster. This modern life may be seen as human innovation and advancement, but the pace of it is increasing our levels of stress. Christians are not immune. In fact, we may be more guilty of overdoing it all because we add church activities to all the things other people do.

In addition to being overly busy and willing to let someone else do the work, we are also growing Biblically illiterate. There were two periods of time when the average Christian knew Scripture well: the Early Church period and the period that was marked by the delivery of the Bible into the language of the common man at the end of the 14th century. Everyone who was literate read the Bible because it was practically the only book available to many. And many put great effort into understanding Christ's teachings. This made the Protestant Reformation possible because the average citizen could recognize errors that the church handed down as "Truth." This attitude toward God's Word prevailed until the early 1900's.

Near the middle of the last century, specialization and busyness conspired against individual Biblical scholarship. We became too busy to fit the Bible into our day. We became too surrounded by the many distractions of our culture and society to see our need for the Bible. And we became specialized to the point of abdicating our responsibility to seek the Scriptures for ourselves. This too is contributing to the church's cultural irrelevance.

These trends are only influences, and do not determine how we live. We can choose to accept cultural influences or to reject them. We are actually no different from Christians of other generations. We all have our culture-specific negative influences to battle. Whether it is conscious or not, we all make our choices. The best way to combat harmful influences is to use a sword - the sword being God's Word. The Word gives us clarity and then conviction. It holds timeless truths for us to see and understand. The scriptures are so rich and deep in wisdom that there are many ways to use the Bible to teach counselors their role. One of my favorite methods is to notice all the times the words "one another" are used in the New Testament. These words are instructions for how to relate with each another. I like to read them altogether to get a snapshot of exactly what we are supposed to be doing. If we are honest, we must admit that many of the cultural activities in which we engage are distractions from what God has given us to do.

The Jar of Rocks

I remember a simple sermon illustration that I saw over fifteen years ago. I have never made an effort to remember it, I just did. The preacher was speaking of the busyness of our lives, and how we often put off serving God until we have finished other things. He reached from under the pulpit and brought out an empty gallon glass jar. He related that the space inside this jar represents the time God has given you in this life. He then, not so carefully, filled the jar with big river rocks. These represent your education. It takes a great deal of time, especially when you are young.

Then he wedged smaller rocks into the jar that slipped down between the larger ones. These represent your career. Or for others, they may represent the time spent racing children around from one activity to the next.

He then sprinkled small gravel into the jar and shook it until the gravel tumbled to the bottom. He continued until not one more piece of gravel would fit into the jar. "These are the recreational activities we love so much, including TV, movies, and time spent on the computer."

Next came sand. He diligently worked the sand into the already full jar until it was flowing out the top. "This is the time we spend with family and friends. It is very important time for us, and we put it into our schedules wherever it might fit."

He then pulled out a large pitcher and poured water that represents the time we spend resting from working so hard to put stuff into our jar! He filled it to the very top. We saw the water filter down into every single space. The jar was on the verge of breaking under the pressure of rocks, gravel, sand and water when he reached down and pulled out a medium sized rock and acted like he was going to push it into the jar. "This is ministry, and I will fit it in somehow!"

Unfortunately he stopped. I wish he would have tried to cram that rock into the jar until it broke. It would have made a stronger impression.

The average American is living at a frantic pace with his life filled to the brim with little time for service and reading scripture. The days of sitting on the front porch and visiting with our neighbors are gone. We now sit inside or may venture to our secluded back yard surrounded by a tall fence. We pull into our garage and close the door of our fortress with a button. We enter our cocoon and dive into the things that we have made important: television programs, internet activities, hobbies, etc. We suddenly look at a clock and realize the evening is over and we need to prepare for tomorrow. We hit the sack, not even noticing that we didn't communicate care and concern for one person, sometimes not even the people with whom we share our homes. A TIME magazine poll from 2006 showed that out of 11 categories of personal activities, caring for someone outside of the household was tenth. Watching TV came in second, losing only to sleep.

Our Most Defining Relationship

The word "self" is used more often today than ever before: self esteem, self actualization, self awareness, true to self, self fulfilled, self sufficient, self, self, self. With all the focus on self-help literature and workshops, you would think everyone would be self fulfilled, but sadly we are not. Something is very wrong with this "self" focus. Jesus taught the exact opposite. He taught,

> "Whoever wants to be my disciple must deny themselves and take up their cross and follow me" (Luke 9:23).

Paul advises not to think more highly of yourself than you ought, and to put off the old self and put on the new self, "which is being renewed in knowledge in the image of its Creator" (Ephesians 4:22). James said in Chapter 1:22-25,

> "Do not merely listen to the word, and so deceive yourselves. Do what it says. Anyone who listens to the word but does not do what it says is like a man who looks at his face in a mirror and, after looking at himself, goes away and immediately forgets what he looks like. But the man who looks intently into the perfect law that gives freedom, and continues to do this, not forgetting what he has heard, but doing it—he will be blessed in what he does."

This verse teaches that we can look at ourselves as long as we are looking through God's word for the purpose of putting it into action.

I have noticed that the individual who focuses on the self, seems to have a chronic problem with low self esteem. It is odd but true. We perceive our value from our most significant relationship. If that relationship is with yourself, then what you think of yourself defines your value. If your most significant relationship is with your spouse, then his or her opinion will determine your idea of your self worth. Both of these options can be unstable and potentially negative. But if we look toward God and keep Him as our most significant relationship, then He will define our value. He is consistent and sent His Son to die because we are valued by Him. Whatever happens in our world or whatever anyone may say or do to us, we can be safe and sure of our value.

What is Our Territory?

I have met many people who are thrilled about Christian peer counseling. Both believers and nonbelievers are supportive of the ministry. On the other hand, I have also met those who do not believe counseling should be a part of "church work." They believe counseling is exclusively for trained professionals, and what is done among Christians in small groups and in prayer meetings should not be considered counseling. I strongly oppose this thinking for many reasons. The greatest support for Christian peer counseling comes from scripture and it is there in abundance. Some believers and even Christian leaders are more comfortable with the terms "mentoring" or "spiritual coaching." These things occur naturally in a healthy church environment, but so does counseling. I realize the very term "counseling" can be a bit elusive and the term means different things to different people. Regardless of the definition, counseling is squarely in the domain of Christianity and has been long before colleges and universities began to offer degrees with that title.

There are forces from without and forces from within the church that are working against the idea of Christian peer counseling. The forces from outside our walls are easier for us to understand and combat. We know we are in a battle with the world around us and that the Christian walk is a narrow path. But as Christians, we are more easily blind-sided by internal influences. We are soothed into complacency without being cognizant of it. There is a genuine spiritual battle around us that has raged from the beginning, and will continue to the end. As Christian peer counselors, you are front line soldiers, so be aware of the battle and be safe in it.

Chapter 4

The Book of Proverbs for Peer Counselors and Mentors

*"Being a good counselor and a good listener is one
of the most selfless things you will ever do."*

Author Unknown

This chapter is built from the wisdom found in Proverbs and a few other books scattered through the Holy Scriptures. These books represent only a microcosm of the vast wisdom contained in the Bible. I hope to impart wisdom by sharing these few scriptures, but I also hope you will seek a more complete understanding by reading the Bible in its entirety. There is no equal to the wisdom found in the Bible and a lifetime is too short to comprehend its wealth.

My goal is to demystify the whole idea of counseling. Before I knew better, I believed that the experts, the elite few, possess some sort of mysterious knowledge about the soul of men. They had an unexplained ability to change people. These experts held knowledge that commoners did not have. Later, I discovered that these beliefs are not altogether true. The real things that help people to change and to grow are not hidden or mysterious at all. In fact, the answers to most of our perplexing modern problems have been in front of our noses and have been there for thousands of years. Consider the following verses from Psalms and Proverbs:

"I will bless the Lord who has counseled me. Indeed, my mind instructs me in the night. I have set the Lord continually before me: because He is at my right hand, I will not be shaken" (Psalm 16:7-8).

"He who trusts in himself is a fool, but he who walks in wisdom is kept safe"(Proverbs 28-26).

"He who conceals his sins does not prosper, but whoever confesses and renounces them finds mercy" (Proverbs 28:13).

These scriptures all speak of our relationship with God. Before we can reach out to someone else, we must be anchored firmly with the Lord ourselves. This is the first and perhaps the greatest nugget of wisdom from Proverbs; we must first hear His voice and His counsel before we can teach someone else.

It is also imperative that our relationship with our Creator remains current and fresh. As David wrote in Psalm 16, "I have set the Lord continually before me." It is easy to fall behind with God and fail to bring our daily concerns to Him. It is a continual process to confess, to praise, to rededicate ourselves and to ask for help in keeping our intimacy with Him. It is possible to consistently attend church and serve God without knowing Him well. Some believers walk around with a stale faith, a faith that is not up to date and current with God. Some have a faith that is all on the outside and have not let Him into their hearts where they feel and truly live. My prayer is that this chapter speaks to you deeply and you will let God dwell in every part of you. He wants to be in your doubts, fears, victories and failures. It is hard to believe, but God wants all parts of you, even the ugly and despicable parts because He knows that they will keep us away from Him. He is not interested in a future version of you, He is interested in you as you are now. More than anything, he wants to know us and to relate to us. A proficient peer counselor is truly *alive in Christ*. Some of the things people tell you may be upsetting and disturbing. You may not be prepared to hear of tragedies, abuse, and other experiences. But if you are alive in Christ, you will not be shaken. If the core of who you are is anchored in Christ, the winds may blow and the waters rise, but the foundation will not fail. These, I pray, are not just words of wisdom from the Proverbs, but living words that penetrate into the place where God lives in you.

Be Attentive and Listen

There is a time to speak when we are counseling, and there is a time to remain quiet. It requires wisdom to know when to do each. It is my experience and observation that most people talk too soon when counseling or mentoring. The listening part must come first. This might seem obvious, but in most conversations people will listen for only about ten seconds before they start thinking or talking about themselves, or even offering advice. Our words are more meaningful once we have first logged in the time listening. The following scriptures from Proverbs and the book of James address the importance of listening and not reacting immediately.

"...Everyone should be quick to listen, slow to speak and slow to become angry" (James 1:19).

"A fool shows his annoyance at once, but a prudent man overlooks an insult" (Proverbs 12:16).

"A man of knowledge uses words with restraint, and a man of understanding is even-tempered" (Proverbs 17:27).

"He who answers before listening-that is his shame" (Proverbs 18:23).

"A fool gives full vent to his anger, but a wise man keeps himself under control" (Proverbs 29:11).

If I made a pie chart illustrating the proportion of the time a good counselor is listening in a counseling session, listening would nearly cover the entire chart. Only during a small amount of the time are we actually speaking. As time passes, we may need to increase the amount of information we share, but the vast majority of time should comprise listening, reflecting and offering occasional questions. Many times, those who I am counseling do not at first reveal their true reason for seeking help. They wait and test me to determine if I am really going to take the time to listen and show them that I care. People are cautious with their personal feelings and information until they know that you are safe and are not going to judge and quickly try to "solve" their problems. It is insulting to another person to have the answers to their life's questions ready so quickly. In my first appointment, even if I believe I know what the problems are and how to fix them, I resist this trap of blurting out my opinions. I need to go deeper and be more curious about them. It takes time, sometimes a great deal of time, to grasp who they really are and what they truly need.

In the mid 1980's I attended a small Christian college located in the heart of Nebraska. This college recruited new students by sending some of their current students to summer Bible camps. I was one of a handful of students given the honor of representing our fine college as a recruiter for the summer.

The college paired me with another student, gave us a car and a gas card and sent us off to 11 weeks of camps throughout the mid-west. Our job was simply to show up at each camp, do whatever the camp staff asked of us for the week and talk to the campers about our college as time allowed. We traveled to Colorado, South Dakota, Illinois, Indiana, Minnesota and Kansas.

One particular trip between camps was especially long. We had just finished a camp in South Dakota and were traveling to Muncie, Indiana, which was about an 18 to 20 hour drive. We were young and ambitious, so we drove straight through and arrived in Muncie about 5:00 am. Neither of us had been to Indiana, we did not know a single person in the area and, unfortunately, did not know the location of the camp. Even though it was still early in the morning we decided to call the camp director, Max, to get directions to the camp so we could get a few precious hours of sleep before the excited young campers arrived.

Max was glad to hear from us, even at such an early hour, and kindly gave us a long list of highway numbers and turns to the remote location of the camp. He also gave us directions to his house in the event we could not find the camp and instructed us to go into the house without waking him and his family.

After an hour of driving on Indiana country roads in the dark, we gave up our search for the camp and followed the directions to his house. The front door was locked, so we entered through the back, used the restroom, passed on the temptation to raid the refrigerator and crashed on the floor in the living room.

It wasn't five minutes later that a lady came down the stairs of this very nice Victorian house and stated, "I'm glad I had my clothes on." She quickly scampered upstairs to return almost immediately with her husband. We sluggishly, but politely, introduced ourselves. We did not even bother to get out of our sleeping bags, and I lay down after our introductions and tried to get to sleep.

To my dismay, the couple continued talking with my partner. Didn't they know how far we had just driven and that we had been up all night? My partner continued talking with them until I had a most uncomfortable and disturbing thought. I sat up and asked the gentleman if his name was Max. He politely said, "No." We were in Max's neighbor's house! Oops!

Looking back, my mistake was not listening better to Max's instructions. I was sure I knew what to do, what course to take, but I was wrong. We have to be careful about thinking we know the answers too quickly, because we may be in the wrong house completely.

So how do you know when to say something? Listening is a substantial part of counseling, but there is a time to speak. Here are a few more verses to consider.

> "A gentle answer turns away wrath, but a harsh word stirs up anger. The tongue that brings healing is a tree of life, but a deceitful tongue crushes the spirit. The lips of the wise spread knowledge; not so the hearts of fools" (Proverbs 15:1-7).

Our words can be powerful, especially after we have showed someone that we care by listening to them.

Part of counseling may be confronting sin, bringing light to a lie, pointing out discrepancies in a story, or admonishing about false beliefs regarding themselves or others. But when should you bring these things up? How do you know when to do it? A practical rule to follow is that *you can confront only as much as you have supported.* For example, a couple that is living together may seek counsel concerning their relationship. You could begin by telling them they are living in sin and living outside of God's plan. That probably won't be heard and they will likely not return. Or you could listen and empathize with the struggles they are experiencing, offer words of encouragement, and spend time understanding what kind of people they are and what they desire for their relationship. Then after connecting well with them you can leverage some of the trust you have built. At this point they are much more likely to consider anything you say because you have built a relationship and earned their trust. During an appointment with one of our peer counselors, a client said, "You have to earn the right to speak to me that way." It was a friendly way to tell the counselor that he had moved to the confrontation too soon.

The Flour Bomb War

There are few people alive today who can tell of personal experiences in flour bomb wars. I am one of them.

As a teenager, I attended a local Christian camp. The camp had a wide age range from grade school to high school seniors. The most anticipated part of this week-long camp was "The Flour Bomb War!"

The war was a version of a camp activity called capture-the-flag. Since the camp was located in Colorado, there was a demand to give extra grit and drama, or I should say, flour and drama to the game.

There were two teams: the attackers and the defenders. The game was a strong competitive activity held in a beautiful narrow, wooded canyon with a picturesque rushing creek in the middle of it. These natural features gave the war its boundaries.

Flour bombs were the ammunition. They were made by putting a tablespoon of flour into a thin facial tissue, then the four corners were tied with a rubber band. When the flour bomb was accurately thrown at a fellow camper it would break, spilling flour all over the victim. A floured camper indicated he or she was "dead." When the camper was hit with a bomb, he was considered a casualty, and had to surrender any remaining bombs in his possession. He was then escorted to the neutral area out of action. Each child had about six or seven bombs to last the entire war.

Since I was one of the oldest at the camp, I was selected to be one of the two generals in command. My team was the attackers. Our objective was to fight our way down the canyon and capture the flag by removing it from its place inside a circle. If we accomplished this within a specified time period, we would win the war. The defenders did everything in their power to stop us.

As a general, my strategy was all about deception. The enemy was going to be deceived as well as my own forces. I was instructed to use everyone on my team, regardless of their size and interest (or lack thereof) in the war. The smaller children, numbering about seven or eight, were convincingly told to storm down the small jeep trail and get the flag. They were little and quick, but I knew the enemy would be expecting an attack up the road and had planned accordingly.

In former years, the enemy had dragged dead trees in the road to slow the attackers. This diversion gave them an easy chance to flour bomb the attackers into oblivion.

These innocent kids did not know what they were up against. They were my pawns and I was using them in a diversion tactic to attract the enemy's attention and, hopefully, make them use up their ammunition. I did not want my diversion force to know that they had no chance to survive the attackers. It was a deceptive suicide mission and a cruel reality of war.

The girls, who generally thought the war to be "stupid," would go up the creek making a lot of noise to deceive the enemy into believing that the main force was advancing toward the flag from the creek. But unknown to the enemy, as well as to most of my team, was the secret plan of attack. A couple of older boys and I were going to hike up the side of the mountain and come down behind enemy forces to get the flag. Late in the war the bombs would be few, the enemy would be concentrating on the two diversions, and we would be the heroes. I impressed myself with the brilliance of my plan.

The defense team took off and had a few minutes to set up their strategy. We were given the go ahead and the war began. The children took off on their suicide mission and the girls went toward the creek making noise and talking loudly, a skill at which they were naturally adept.

We advanced up the hill on our covert mission to win the war. We climbed for several minutes up the hillside covered with trees and unusually thick brush. No one suspected our advance because this route was well beyond where the enemy would believe any sane attacker would venture.

The sounds of the flour bomb war were heard in the distance: shouting, laughing and screaming. The time quickly came for our descent. We skillfully made our way to the flag area and found, to our surprise, that the flag was not there. Everyone was standing around eating watermelon. The war was over. We were stunned!

Something had gone terribly wrong. I stood in disbelief, all scratched up from a not so heroic climb. The little kids did the impossible. They made it all the way down the jeep trail, over the barriers, through enemy lines and captured the flag, exactly like their general had told them. They did not know it was impossible. They had no idea it was a suicide mission with zero chance of success. It was done out of faith in my words.

What a lesson I learned! Words are extremely powerful and I need to be careful what I say to people. A kind word, a careless comment - all go deep and are taken to heart.

God gives us many instructions on how we are to speak to one another because it is important. Words are powerful tools for good or evil. We need to be especially careful when giving advice and direction. We must be prayerful and thoughtful about what we say. Here are a few of the many verses to consider.

"Reckless words pierce like a sword, but the tongue of the wise brings healing" (Proverbs 12:18).

"A prudent man keeps his knowledge to himself, but the heart of fools blurts out folly"

(Proverbs 12:23).

"An anxious heart weighs a man down, but a kind word cheers him up" (Proverbs 12:25).

"Even a fool is thought wise if he keeps silent, and discerning if he holds his tongue"

(Proverbs 17:28).

"A fool finds no pleasure in understanding but delights in airing his own opinions"

(Proverbs 18:2).

"He who answers before listening, that is his shame" (Proverbs 18:13).

There is a time to speak when we are counseling. But be sure you have first gained their trust or they will not hear you. It is better to err on the side of giving too little advice than to give too much advice, too early.

Be Selfless, Not Needy

"We make a living by what we get but we make a life by what we give."

Winston Churchill

The bottom line is that counseling, mentoring or life coaching is not about you, it is about the person to whom you are listening. Being a good counselor and a good listener is one of the most selfless things you will ever do.

"... Jesus said to his disciples, 'If anyone would come after me, he must deny himself and take up his cross and follow me" (Matthew 16:24).

In graduate school, we were sitting around one day contemplating ourselves. Each of us shared the reasons we wanted to be counselors. All of them revolved around our desires to make a difference in the world or how we wanted to help people change.

Although these are noble causes, I believe they are precursors to failure. What if the person you are counseling actually gets worse? Proverbs 1:28-32 teaches of people who "did not choose to fear the Lord…waywardness of the simple will kill them and the complacency of fools will destroy them…" Some people are hell-bent on destroying their lives, their marriages and their children. They appear to be normal, successful people and may come with great awareness and ambition to change, but they don't. If you are in the counseling relationship to change them, you are going to feel just as miserable as they do. Our feelings cannot be tied to our ability to rescue someone. It is God's job to rescue, not ours.

"A hot-tempered man must pay the penalty; if you rescue him, you will have to do it again" (Proverbs 19:19).

"When the storm has swept by, the wicked are gone, but the righteous stand firm forever" (Proverbs 10:25).

One of the most prominent themes in Proverbs is the contrast between those who are wise and those who are foolish. The wise are seeking, listening and gaining great rewards. The foolish are proud, lazy, and selfish. Sometimes the penalty must be paid for foolishness and we see it unfold right in front of us. We cannot be responsible for their success or failure. We offer listening ears and encouraging words of wisdom, but they must choose whether to accept them.

The better reason to provide counsel is that it is *the right thing to do*. I have had many sessions where hope seems to be lost, and I cannot seem to do anything to help. But I can leave these appointments feeling that I have provided the best possible counseling I could. God sent me, I went and I gave it my all. This keeps me going and going – like a bunny beating a drum. What they do with my counsel is their choice. It isn't a harsh or cold feeling; it is the line I draw between them and me.

To illustrate, I can tell you a true story about my friend, Robert. He and his wife were going through some very serious marital difficulties, including several episodes of violence. After a time Robert found the Lord and underwent a radical change. He knew that all trust with his wife had been lost, but for his spiritual walk, he had to change the way he treated her. Among other things, he decided to start giving her flowers, but even that was not easy. He would choose a beautiful bouquet that he thought she would enjoy, he would surprise her with them, and she would immediately throw them into the trash right in front of him. This, of course, hurt his feelings and he became angry.

After he did this a few times, he and his counselor decided on a different approach. He bought the flowers as he did before, but this time he gave them to her and felt secure that as a husband he was loving and nurturing his wife. He focused on his responsibility *to her* and nothing else. As he gave the flowers to her, he reminded himself that if she wanted to throw the flowers in the trash, it was okay because *they were her flowers*.

As you might expect, she threw them in the trash as before but saw that Robert did not have his usual angry reaction. In fact, nothing she did was able to shake his good feeling that he did the right thing for her. The next time Robert gave her flowers she put them in a vase and enjoyed them. Just like Robert, we have to separate ourselves from the outcomes. We can get hurt and our clients might try to manipulate but we must continue to do the right thing.

Some people are on a crash course and nothing you do will change it. They make patterns of poor decisions, and they are not willing to change.

"I love those who love me, and those who seek me find me" (Proverbs 8:14).

Another trap is equally important to avoid. Some people may come to you for help and immediately make improvements. They turn to God, start reading scripture, get baptized and all goes well. Proverbs 2:1-5 states this type of people "…accept words…turning ear to wisdom…call out for insight…cry aloud for understanding…look…search…" Don't take credit for their change, it is a trap. It is the Lord, and it is their open heart, not your ability that facilitated the change.

So whether people change or not, your resolve to serve as a counselor must remain steady. It is not about our need to help or rescue, for we have put ourselves and our wishes on the cross; they ultimately do not matter. My hope is that clients will turn and follow God more closely after they have met with me. But if it doesn't turn out that way, my relationship with God is unchanged because I have done the right thing. It is possible to wish the best for someone, but accept the outcome even if it is not what I had hoped for. Another way to say it is: We are responsible *to* them, but not responsible *for* them.

Be Enthusiastic, Not Over-Religious

"Perfume and incense bring joy to the heart and the pleasantness of one's friend springs from his earnest counsel" (Proverbs 27:9).

"It is not good to have zeal without knowledge, nor be hasty and miss the way" (Proverbs 19:2).

My conversion came from nowhere. I began listening to a local radio program that was aired on a secular rock station on Sunday nights. It was called *Bible Talk* and the preacher of a local church answered questions about life and the Bible live on the air. He was kind, compassionate and very impressive with his knowledge of this book. This program planted the gospel seed in me that matured a year later when I came to the Lord and surrendered my life to Him.

Very soon after that, I sat myself down in church every week and immediately got completely confused. I heard the preacher talk about the New Testament. I had just bought my Bible so I figured it was a New Testament. My Grandma had a really old Bible - at least twenty years old- so I assumed that was an Old Testament. It made complete since to me, but for some reason I could not look up scriptures in either Bible.

To add to my confusion, I did not understand what "chapter" and "verses" were about. I was a high school football player at the time and knew the term "Central Warriors vs. Delta Panthers," and I knew that meant conflict. So when someone said, "Romans 12 verse 2," I heard them say that chapter 12 was "vs." chapter 2. I thought it was some sort of debate going on between parts of the Bible. It seemed like an eternity before I could locate scripture on my own. Christians around me assumed too much when I needed to be taught everything.

After I got the Old and New Testament, and chapters and verses sorted out, I felt inspired to read the Bible. I took someone's advice and started reading the book of Matthew. That went well. Then I started reading Mark, and I was completely confused again. The publishers of my Bible had accidentally put the same pages in my Bible in two different places! I read about Jesus feeding a multitude of people with a small amount of fish and bread and there it was again, that same story. I actually turned back and forth looking for the duplicate page so I could rip it out and fix my Bible. I eventually learned that these books were telling the same story by different accounts. It would have been helpful to know that before I started reading and ripping.

People around me had no idea how "green" I really was to Christian things. We must be careful about this. When people sit down in front of us and say they are Christians or attend church, we cannot assume they know even the basics. Be careful not to use words or phrases they may not understand. We cannot assume they know how to pray or that anyone has ever prayed for them aloud. We cannot conclude they know how to look up a scripture or that they own a Bible. If they have a Bible, we cannot assume they know much about it. If we presume too much, we may confuse them or cause them to feel intimidated and uneasy. My advice is to proceed slowly and always ask permission to pray. Do not use religious words like "redemption," "sanctification," "blood of the lamb," etc. in your prayers because they may have no idea what you mean.

I sat down with a couple from our church who reported to have a marriage problem. I soon learned that the wife had discovered her husband was having sex with a mutual friend. I continued working with them until one of them stopped me and said, "I don't think you understand. We are swingers." I thought, "Well, that's okay because I'm hip and groovy." They had to educate me on what "swinging" was. It is a term used to describe couples who agree to have sex outside of their relationship. The problem was that the husband did not *get permission* to have sex with their friend. I completely misunderstood what they wanted to talk about and I assumed, because they attended church, that they wanted fidelity in their marriage. I'm slow, but I catch on eventually. After they explained what "swingers" do, I was able to begin working with them, as they permitted, regarding their need for God in their lives and for His plan in the marriage.

The Proverbs speak of approaching those we try to help with earnestness and zeal, but with knowledge as well. We need to counsel people where they are. We cannot assume too much. That is why we listen; to learn who they are and where they are in their walk with the Lord.

Be Courageous

"Fear God and have ten-thousand fewer fears."

Unknown

"Our doubts are traitors and make us loose the good we opt might win by fearing to attempt."

William Shakespeare

The things God asks us to do are usually beyond where we feel comfortable and capable. I have met many people who are gifted by God to help others through counseling, but are afraid to try. We have to stretch and grow into His purpose for our lives. It is exciting to discover what He has designed us to do. When we do it, it feels like a little piece of heaven. To be part of God's plan and be part of His will on this earth is our highest calling and the ultimate in earthly satisfaction. It is a true paradox: when you give up your spiritually "safe" position to venture into the uncharted realm to find God's purpose for you, it is only then that you find lasting peace. Let me encourage you to let out what God has put inside of you to do. Share it with a friend. Say it out loud. Pay attention to what makes you come more alive, and then pursue it with all your might.

Unfortunately, the following story is true. It was early autumn in Colorado. The sun was setting, and we were hungry. My wife, Laurie, had gone shopping and was planning to make dinner when she returned. I had stayed home with our small children and decided to surprise her by having dinner completely ready. So I found some chicken breasts and started cooking them. I also found some garlic cloves, chopped them up and put them in the skillet with the chicken. They did not have a lot of flavor, so I put in a little extra and added some other spices. I also made stuffing from a box and a nice green salad. It was a great little dinner, and I had it all ready by the time she returned.

Laurie was surprised and delighted that she did not have to cook dinner that night. We all sat down together and enjoyed my wonderful garlic chicken dinner. As we started cleaning the kitchen, she approached me with a strange look on her face then asked, "What is that in the sink?" When I explained that it was part of the garlic cloves I had chopped up and put in the chicken, she answered, "Those were not garlic cloves. Those were my daffodil bulbs!"

I had cut up and cooked daffodil bulbs, then fed them to my whole family. Earlier that day she had set them on the counter and was planning to plant them in the flower garden at a later time. Then I worried that we all could have been poisoned! Now what do I do? My wife and I were too embarrassed to call anyone to ask, so we went to bed that night a little worried, but otherwise feeling fine. We all woke up the next day in fine health, with a new recipe for daffodil chicken that we will never try again. The moral of the story is to try new things; try something you may not be good at. You most likely will not kill anyone.

I like John Wayne's definition of courage the best: "Courage is being scared to death, but saddling up anyway." It is not the absence of fear that makes us courageous; it is the will to proceed in the presence of fear. Proverbs 3:26 instructs us that the Lord is our confidence. We can rely on Him - the Mighty Counselor - so we can walk into unfamiliar territory. We are the "not so mighty" counselors and should not feel confident if we go into the appointment on our own.

> "Surely the righteous will never be shaken; they
> will be remembered forever. They will have no fear
> of bad news; their hearts are steadfast, trusting in

the LORD. Their hearts are secure, they will have no fear; in the end they will look in triumph on their foes. They have freely scattered their gifts to the poor, their righteousness endures forever; their horn will be lifted high in honor" (Psalm 112:6-9).

"For the Lord will be your confidence and will keep your foot from being snared" (Proverbs 3:26).

"A man cannot be established through wickedness, but the righteous cannot be uprooted"

(Proverbs 12:3).

"The fear of the Lord leads to life: Then one rests content, untouched by troubles" (Proverbs 19:23).

These scriptures provide jewels of wisdom and are very comforting to me. I am naturally shy and find it difficult to walk into a room to talk with people I have never met, people who are expecting me to help them. It takes courage to open that door and introduce myself. I find it much easier to stay home and not venture into personal problems with strangers. But I feel led to do so, and these scriptures are a great solace to me. I am encouraged by these Proverbs that tell of the righteous not being uprooted but resting content, untouched by trouble.

We will certainly hear and witness things we have never been exposed to before. Through others, we will hear of abuse, betrayal and worse, but it does not touch us. We may feel the trauma for a time, but this darkness will not lay a hand on us. We are protected by the Lord. As a shy person I can walk in, sit down and hear about tragedies, adultery and misery and not be affected by it. I feel empathy and love toward others when I hear these stories, but it does not affect the core of who I am or how I feel.

Be Humble

"When pride comes, then comes disgrace, but with humility comes wisdom" (Proverbs 11:2).

"Do you see a man wise in his own eyes? There is more hope for a fool than for him"

(Proverbs 26:12).

"He who trusts in himself is a fool, but he who walks in wisdom is kept safe" (Proverbs 28:26).

Peer counseling will keep you humble if you are paying attention at all. Many times, even as a professional counselor, I call upon the name of the Lord (quietly and to myself of course) right in the middle of a session. I don't always know what to say or what to do. I pray, "God, this is a really good time to do something, because I am totally out of ideas." And he is faithful in answering this prayer because it is prayed from humility and desperation. I enjoy teaching peer counseling to people who do not believe they can do it, because they are more open to God leading them. They listen longer and pray harder.

Be Confidential

"The wise of heart accepts commands, but a chattering fool comes to ruin" (Proverbs 10:8).

"Wisdom is found on the lips of the discerning, but a rod is for the back of him who lacks judgment" (Proverbs 10:13).

"When words are many, sin is not absent, but he who holds his tongue is wise" (Proverbs 10:19).

"A man who lacks judgment derides his neighbor, but a man of understanding holds his tongue" (Proverbs 11:12).

"A gossip betrays a confidence, but a trustworthy man keeps a secret" (Proverbs 11:13).

"He who guards his lips guards his life, but he who speaks rashly will come to ruin"

(Proverbs 13:3).

"A perverse man stirs up dissension, and a gossip separates close friends" (Proverbs 16:28).

"A gossip betrays a confidence; so avoid a man who talks too much" (Proverbs 20:19).

> "If you argue your case with a neighbor, do not betray another man's confidence, or he who hears it may shame you and you will never lose your bad reputation" (Proverbs 25:9-10).

Many of these Proverbs enumerate consequences for betraying confidence or talking too much. This is superb wisdom to remember; the people who come to you and share very personal and meaningful stories are putting their trust in you. If you betray them, they may not trust you again.

Unfortunately, this story is also true. I was working in a counseling center where I did both individual and group counseling. In a group setting, I heard a man's story of his upstairs neighbors keeping him awake until early into the morning. He related that they were loud and were obviously drunk. The group empathized with him and gave him appropriate support and suggestions to help him.

Later that day, a young lady came to me for individual counseling. She reported that she was not feeling well and her medications were not working to control her symptoms. I soon figured out that she was the upstairs neighbor of the man who shared in the group that morning. What a coincidence and an opportunity to find out more about her! I possessed information that she did not know I had.

I asked her if she was getting adequate sleep, and if she had been drinking alcohol. When she answered "No" to both, I knew she was lying. The medications she was taking made it very dangerous for her to drink alcohol. This, in combination with not sleeping at night, was the problem; not solely her medications. I decided to confront. I told her that I knew she had been drinking and staying up very late, but I did not reveal how I knew.

The next morning, when my supervisor called me into his office, I knew I was in some sort of trouble. There, sitting beside his desk, was the man who shared in our group about his sleepless night and partying neighbors. He had just reported to my supervisor that his neighbors threatened him with guns if he ever talked about them again. I broke his confidentiality and he was not happy with me, to say the least. I never anticipated the problems that resulted from using a little information. I did not name a source, but they easily figured it out. This man never did open up much around me again, and I don't blame him. But I did learn a valuable lesson; we must be careful with any bit of information because we never know how people are networked and who they may know. We must be diligent to guard the information we have about others.

A question I often get from new peer counselors is, "What should I do if I encounter the person I am counseling in a store or at church? Should I talk to him, or not?" This situation occurs frequently, even in a large church. It is not just the information they share with you that is confidential. The fact that they are seeing you as a counselor is confidential as well.

I try to match the level of contact they initiate. Sometimes they see me and never look up again. They act as if they do not know me. Don't be offended if this happens to you. We do not know who they might be with and what is going on with them on that particular day. So if this happens, just mirror what they do and continue with your business. (This is a topic you can discuss with them in the first appointment, especially if it is likely that you will see each other or interact in a different setting.) Some people will give you big hugs and introduce you to the world. Most people will smile when they see you, but will not be interested in starting conversations, so that is what I do as well.

Keep Your Boundaries

"Each heart knows its own bitterness, and no one
else can share its joy" (Proverbs 14:10).

This verse highlights our individuality as human beings. We can know a person very intimately, and even be able to anticipate what they may do or think in a given situation, but God sets us apart as individuals. As we interact with others, there are many unspoken rules regarding what is acceptable behavior between us. In addition, each individual relationship we have has a different set of rules of behavior or *boundaries.*

A counseling relationship is unique to any other relationship and the boundaries are unique as well. We must grow close to those to whom we listen and desire to help, but must *also* keep a healthy separation from them. Emotionally, we can engage with them but let them go after our time with them is complete. This is truly a challenging dance. We have close access to very personal information, yet have some distance from interacting with them on a daily basis. We know details about their life experiences, but must remain objective.

As counselors and mentors we have a responsibility to give sound and helpful feedback. This feedback comes from our emotional and intellectual reaction to their stories. Ideally, we reach a place in our counseling relationship where we have a close emotional connection, but are able to still reason in such a way to give them logical and practical feedback. This can be tricky, to say the least.

The "information sheet" found in chapter 11 is an effective way to set boundaries at the beginning of the relationship. Share this form with them. We have often found in peer counseling dynamics that "clients" want to become our friends. They are interested in interacting with us in casual settings and we are often invited to visit them at their homes or to join them at restaurants for meals. This situation frequently arises and I let each provider decide individually how to handle this situation.

As a professional counselor, I can set firm boundaries due to the professional/client relationship. I say, "Because of this special relationship I have with you, I am not able to see you personally as a friend. I want to keep my objectivity in this relationship." Something similar could be said if you are asked to be a friend and you choose not to accept. Peer counseling is a little different in that you do not have "professional relationships" with clients. But you may still set boundaries for relationships so you can uniquely offer an objective perspective.

Some peer counselors have befriended their clients. I do not object to this, but I do offer a word of caution: if this happens with everyone you counsel, it will not be long before you have too many friends. When someone desires to befriend you when you are his peer counselor, it may be diagnostic that he is having trouble establishing meaningful relationships in his life. This may be an opportunity to search for what is hindering him from establishing relationships in natural settings outside of counseling. I believe it is better to help people grow to a point where they are able to find their own friends rather than fulfilling this need ourselves.

Peer counselors have accepted invitations to meet with their clients at restaurants as a way to accept gifts of thanks for their time and efforts. It is nice to be appreciated, and it is an enjoyable way to close the counseling relationship, but keep in mind your unique position of being an objective helper, and for most counselors a personal distance is necessary to maintain objectivity.

Expect Blessings

Counseling is about self sacrifice and taking up your cross to be able to completely listen and show empathy for another person. But like any service to God, there are rewards that are greater than anything we can give. This is especially true of peer counseling. Consider the following Proverbs:

"A generous man will prosper; he who refreshes others will himself be refreshed" (Proverbs 11:25).

"A man finds joy in giving an apt reply- and how good is a timely word" (Proverbs 15:23).

As the Proverbs indicate, the spiritual reward we receive as peer counselors and mentors is truly refreshing for our souls. We give our time and attention to someone who is hurting. God recognizes our efforts and sends us joy that is often unexpected, but so energizing.

Our Father shows His character in many ways through scripture. One example that especially demonstrates His character is the story of Jesus giving the disciples a fishing lesson. They had been fishing in their boats all night and had not caught anything. I'm not sure they knew that it was Him at the time, but from the shore He instructed them to cast their nets on the other side of the boat. They complied with this absurd request and what happened next illustrates God's character. He blessed them with a catch so large that, "...they signaled their partners in the other boat to come and help them, and they came and filled both boats so full that they began to sink" (Luke 5:7). God could have given a catch that was just enough, or above average, but instead He drove an enormous amount of fish into the nets so that they had more than they could handle and had to call for reinforcements to accept the blessings.

This indicates something about His nature. God is excited about giving us blessings and His blessings are wonderful and filling to our souls. Besides moments of singing and worship, I have never experienced this overfilling joy or seen it in others in greater measure than when God uses and blesses someone who serves others. In caring for souls, God will bless you so much that you have to share the blessing with others because it is so overwhelming that you need help to receive it all.

Be Tenacious

"A man of many companions may come to ruin, but there is a friend who sticks closer than a brother" (Proverbs 18:24).

Those who have played with me may not agree, but I am actually pretty good at golf. In fact, in every single game I have played, I have been able to get that ball in all eighteen holes! The only problem I have ever encountered with the game is that some players insist on counting the strokes it takes to get the ball into the hole. Eventually I get it in, so why keep track? In the absence of every other great quality, tenacity more than compensates.

As a peer counselor, you may not believe that you have exceptional counseling skills or personal experiences that will bring insight to the people seeking help from you. But if you just stick with them, God will bless both of you.

Who is King of the Jungle?

There once was a young lion who had recently learned that he was now the oldest male lion in the jungle. As he strutted through the jungle, He thought to himself, "I am now king of this entire jungle. King over all other animals!" He felt very proud.

Seeking confirmation of his greatness he strolled up to Giraffe and asked, "Who is king of the jungle?"

Knowing Lion was physically stronger and had sharper teeth, Giraffe quickly answered, "Lion, you are supreme king of the jungle, no question about it." This was exactly what he was looking for, but he yearned for yet more confirmation.

He found the old and wise Hippopotamus. "Hippopotamus, who is the king of the jungle?"

"You are, of course, my great king," Hippopotamus replied, just wanting to be left alone. Now Lion was feeling more confident than ever, but still needed more.

This young Lion approached the mighty elephant, "Who is king of the jungle?"

With a mean glare in his eye, Elephant wrapped his trunk around Lion's neck, strangling him until he turned blue. He threw him way up into the air to the top of a giant tree. The "King of the Jungle" bashed into branches as he came crashing to the ground. Elephant kicked with both of his hind legs, sending the Lion tumbling over boulders, into cactus and through thorn bushes. Elephant casually walked over to Lion, who was now completely defenseless, grabbed him again with his trunk, and for good measure, beat him against a tree, then threw him into the water hole. The dazed and nearly dead Lion said, with the only strength he had left, "You don't have to get so mad because you don't know the answer."

This story reminds me how fixed people can be in their troubles and how blind they can be to the truth. Arrogance, independence, a long history of denial; all can leave a person nearly blind to a way out.

Many times, you are the only person holding hope for them. Every other person has belittled, abused, betrayed or given up on them. They may fail repeatedly and seem to be blind to the truth that there is hope for them. But people do change, they do see the light - sometimes slowly, very slowly. God's love is tenacious and we must be also.

Chapter 5
Supernatural Relationships

"There is much suffering in the world - very much. Material suffering is suffering from hunger, suffering from homelessness, from all kinds of disease, but I still think that the greatest suffering is being lonely, feeling unloved, just having no one."

Mother Teresa

This is what peer counseling and mentoring are all about; not letting someone be alone. We make ourselves available to be with them, to listen to everything: the sin, the suffering, the painful parts of the story. We are there not to judge, condemn, or laugh and mock like so many people have. We are there to hear the whole story to the end. This is the cure for the greatest of human suffering, and it is supernatural.

What is the difference between an ordinary relationship and a supernatural relationship? We think of the supernatural as something that is miraculous, or maybe even weird. I think of unexplained physical healing, words of prophesy, or multiplying food for thousands. But what about the supernatural when it becomes common? We observe it so often that we do not see it for what it really is; God working in our lives. I think this is true for supernatural relationships. We become so familiar with God working in our relationships that the supernatural becomes familiar and can be dismissed as ordinary.

It takes keen observation to see Him work, but He does work and I have witnessed it many times. I have been part of supernatural moments in counseling and have left these appointments knowing that God had visited all of us in the room. At other times, I am convinced that my client and I were brought together supernaturally for a divine purpose, a purpose that was set by Him for us to accomplish. These moments are astonishing to me and keep me laboring as a counselor with great thankfulness and eagerness for more.

Many of the participants in our ministry tell me of these supernatural experiences as well. The next few chapters are dedicated to describing what I believe are the best ways to bring God into the counseling session, or rather, how to cooperate with God's Spirit who is already at work.

Before we journey into the mysteries of God's power and how He may work in our counseling, I would like to first cover a topic that is absolutely necessary for the peer counselor to understand. Before a supernatural relationship is possible we must listen. Not only listen, but do so at a divine level. Anyone can casually listen to the radio or the TV or to another person. But as hard as we try, our own thoughts and opinions come crashing through and we begin to relate everything that is said to our own experiences. Before long we are thinking about ourselves and are no longer completely listening.

How can we avoid the interference from our own head and go deeper when listening to someone else? How can we avoid getting distracted? How can we train our attention to the degree that the relationship has the potential to move into the supernatural? The answer, of course, is that only God can take us into a deeper level of relating. It is a mystery how all of this actually happens, but our part is simple: listen.

The selfless part of the experience is the most challenging. Human beings have the hardest time keeping themselves from taking center stage. Jesus was not selfish and was able to focus on others better than anyone else ever has. While others were talking, he was not thinking about what was best for himself, or what he needed to say to sound smart, or how he could or could not relate to the person. He listened with the other person's eternity in mind.

The gospels do not tell of Jesus relating to people on a superficial level. I imagine He may have enjoyed casually chatting about the weather, but what is recorded is that He cut through the crust, the posing, the pretending, the distractions and went right into the heart of the person; where the fears and hopes live.

One reason he could do this was that he had a true gift of knowledge. He knew people at the deepest level and even knew things about them that he did not learn from them. For example, He knew about the relationships of the woman at the well and how many relationships she had. From my understanding of scripture, He did not learn this from her. He knew this because He was God.

Not having the gift of knowledge myself, I must listen and build a relationship with a person to gain important information. If we are to know how many marriages someone had, we have to listen when he or she tells us. If we are to know someone at the depth necessary to help him grow, we must build trust and understanding over time. There is no short cut. Listening is our greatest tool to connect with others on a supernatural level.

The following information is presented so we can study and practice listening until we master the skill. Only then can we be part of the cure for the greatest of human suffering: loneliness.

1. Simple Listening

People want to see and hear you listening. Listening to someone is one of the most interesting of all human behaviors. Listening is a skill that most people do not practice. I have observed in casual conversations that most people will listen for about ten seconds before they start talking. We love to talk about ourselves and give our opinions. Listening is one of the most selfless things that we can do for someone else, but it is not something we naturally do well.

Listening is more than just remaining quiet and paying attention to what is said, it is being intent on understanding. You must **show the person that you are listening** and that you comprehend what he is saying. This is called "active listening." This is a critical skill for any counselor. How well you listen will influence the outcome of counseling more than anything else you can do. What is considered good listening in our everyday lives will not work for us as counselors and mentors. Some counselors and mentors have unknowingly sent strong negative messages to those they are trying to help. Be humble and consider how you are being perceived. Practice the following skills. They may seem trivial, but let me assure you, they are important and powerful. Some people have even developed their listening skills to the degree that it is a form of art. In fact, I see listening as an art form rather than a skill. It is like dancing: it is a beautiful thing to behold, especially if you are on the receiving end.

Eye contact is our strongest way to communicate. Paul tells us in the first chapter of Ephesians that the eyes are the window of the soul. There is so much to learn by looking into the eyes, but we must be careful not to overdo it with too much eye contact. A good rule to follow is to match the eye contact they give to you. Some people will not look up much at all while others will practically stare a hole through your head. Mirror whatever they do.

Open and forward body position tells people we are interested in them. You may be able to hear them just as well while leaning back in your chair with your arms crossed, but they would most likely get the message that you are not interested in what they are saying and, in fact, may see you as judgmental. Crossing the legs does not send a strong negative message, but it is something to consider. The ideal position is to sit up straight or to lean slightly forward. Observe people around you and be aware of what they do to make you feel relaxed while you are speaking. These are the same behaviors you must show others so they will feel comfortable to share with you. We must do everything in our power to convey that we care and are going to listen.

Head nods and minimal verbal responses make a big difference. If you sit perfectly still and quiet, they will likely stop talking or feel uncomfortable. They need to know they are being heard. Some counselors/mentors naturally say "uh huh" and "hmm" and nod their heads up and down like plastic dogs in car windows, but some of us need to make conscious efforts to do these simple things. Some other verbal responses like, "Tell me more," "Go ahead," and "That's interesting," are simple nondirective encouragement for the person to keep sharing.

All of these simple behaviors may be more powerful than you realize. If you neglect these skills, you will be missing great opportunities to go deeper. Most people are not accustomed to having someone show complete interest in what they are saying and will talk almost uncontrollably when they know they have an interested audience.

2. Reflections

When we look at ourselves in a mirror, we see only what is there and nothing else. It is a reflection of our image with nothing added. Even though a little enhancement may be beneficial, it is the reality of your image that you see. The same is the goal for reflection in the counseling relationship. We want to reflect only what the person tells us. At this stage, we are the mirror and nothing more. Later we will carefully input information, but initially the goal is to reflect only what is said and meant.

One simple way to reflect is to offer **restatements.** This is simply restating and/or summarizing what the person said. I know none of you eat fast food, but if you did, you would hear a great example of restatement. The employee taking the order must communicate accurately to keep the people moving through the line and the profits flowing in. After taking the order, the worker repeats it back to you. If it is not correct, you and the employee keep working at it until you are getting exactly what you desire. Counseling is no different. You must keep restating until they are accurately understood.

Don't feel badly if you restate incorrectly and must be corrected in your understanding. This is a sign that the relationship is growing to the point that accurate communication is important. At times, a person gets very involved in telling his story because it is the first time someone has really put forth effort to understand him. You may need to slow him down by saying something like, "Let me see if I understand what you are saying. You said. . ." This lets both him and you know that you understand accurately. And more than just assuring that the communication is precise, it helps the two of you connect and takes the conversation to greater depths.

Summary statements are also effective tools. At times the client will talk for a long time without pausing to allow you to restate. I sometimes will say, "Hold on for just a minute, let me see if I understand what you said." And then I try to summarize in a short paragraph back to them. This accomplishes several things. It slows the client down to a workable pace and lets him/her know you want to understand completely.

The next level of reflection is *reflection of feeling*. This often takes a person into deeper levels of relating. If the session time is nearly over, then I must be careful not to reflect feelings because once a person goes deeper into his feelings you can't cut him off suddenly. Many times he may not be able to identify his feelings and may not be able to express his emotions in words. We must help him identify his feelings by "fishing" for just the right words. When the feeling is correctly identified and restated, a light goes on, a connection is made and loneliness is averted. This simple process is extremely powerful in building a relationship with another person. When you connect at a feeling level, it brings a closeness that many people lack in their lives. Many times this connection with you is all they need.

Another great tool for listening is *reflection of process*. This can be extremely beneficial, but it is not easy to do. It is a summary of what you see happening. For example, you might say, "What I have heard you talk about for the past few weeks is that you see yourself as being persecuted by others in your life," or "I hear your comments about your wife and none of them seem to be complimentary." These are not simply restatements of what you have heard, but are noticeable *themes* the clients are communicating. A ten dollar word for this is "metacommunication," which means to communicate about the communication. It can be very valuable to the client to have someone reflect the larger focus of the problem. As human beings, it is difficult to see this wide-angle view of ourselves. Good listeners will reflect words as they go, but also be able to summarize and reflect the themes and patterns in clients' stories.

The deepest level of reflection is called *deep affective reflection.* This is simply feeling what clients are feeling at the same moment in time that they do. This unmistakably shows them that you understand what they mean. This is not something you say, it is something that both of you feel. For example, at times I may tear up while my client is speaking. I am struck emotionally by something he says or I am picking up on a feeling he is experiencing. This response from me brings out more of the feeling in clients. It is as if the feeling is bouncing back and forth between the two of us. This validates the truth of the experience in a powerful way with no words needed. This does not happen in every session or with every person, but when it does it is usually a true healing experience.

Any of these techniques can be improved with practice. Try it with your friends. I have also practiced while driving and listening to the radio. I hear lyrics in a song, then turn the volume down while I restate. It is enjoyable and teaches your ears to really tune into the content and feelings of what is said.

Being a good listener requires energy and attention. Please keep in mind that listening is not for the lazy, the selfish or the overly busy. It takes effort and security in the Lord to effectively sit and listen. To not think about yourself, to not judge, and to not be afraid of failure takes confidence, or what I call "Godfidence." Have faith that God is with you and that nothing is beyond His power to heal. When we have this Godfidence we can be calm in our spirits and be part of a three-way supernatural relationship with our client and the Lord God.

Chapter 6
Spirit Focused Counseling: The Foundation

"It's not about counseling, it's about the miraculous work of the One who loves us."

> Scott Holzschuh,
> Marriage Mentor

Anytime we try to understand God's Holy Spirit, we are reminded of the great mystery surrounding Him. He has infinite wisdom and we do not. Our minds and hearts can see glimpses of His glory, but cannot fathom Him in His entirety.

> "Now to Him who is able to do immeasurably more than all we ask or imagine according to His power that is at work within us, to him be glory in the church and in Christ Jesus throughout all generations, for ever and ever! Amen"
>
> (Ephesians 3:20-21).

God is working in our lives and able to accomplish more than we can imagine. I cannot put into words nor can I completely grasp what God's Spirit does in my life. He really can do more than we can fathom if we get out of His way and allow Him to use *"His power that is at work within us."*

The following is my understanding of the way God works through counseling. Everyone who counsels and mentors works from some sort of model, even if he does not realize it. A model is simply a way to think about and use information. The model I am presenting is Biblical and Holy Spirit based as much as I can present it. Most of the counseling models taught and used today are humanistic, which means they do not accept the authority of scriptures or recognize or accept God's help. They trust in human wisdom and ambition alone to direct their efforts.

By human ambition, a dysfunctional behavior can be stopped only to be replaced by another. Addictions are traded for different addictions. For example, a person who has relationship difficulties may delve into books, therapy, etc. to gain self insight to the degree that the pursuit of knowledge about himself becomes a problem. Many alcoholics have become addicted and dependent on recovery rather than dependent on God. Without seeking the help of the Holy Spirit mental health professionals can only teach their clients coping skills rather than teach them how to live fully, and have a relationship with the Author of Life.

Even many Christian models of counseling are simply secular models with scriptures added to give them a Christian feel. Their foundations are not built from scripture but are built on faith in human strength rather than God's strength. To deny the Spirit His role is damaging and grossly counterproductive.

Some Christian models use scripture as an agent for change, but do not consider the work of the Holy Spirit. They use scripture memorization and teach from The Word, believing that is the only way God works. They do not believe that the Holy Spirit arranges circumstances, speaks to them with audible words or impressions, or directs their lives in specific ways. For them, God works through the written word, and through it exclusively. This approach denies the Spirit His full role.

Other Christian models accept the work of the Holy Spirit but are weak in the use of scripture. Many of my Christian clients are amazingly inept at knowing and using God's word. Modern Christian culture, I fear, is growing more illiterate. Many do not know scripture well and base their faith and their walk with God on what others tell them about scripture. Their understanding is shallow because they don't go to the inspired source to study for themselves.

I believe we must base our counseling model, and our lives for that matter, on knowledge and use of God's word AND dependence and relationship with God's active Holy Spirit. We need both for our model and our lives to be complete.

Truth #1 - God Must Be the Changing Agent

Over the past one hundred years, Western secular psychologists have developed models to understand the world and to guide their work to help others through their problems. I think it is necessary to mention some of these models in broad historical categories because they have become part of our thinking, even if we do not realize it. I do not wish to frame them as evil or bad, but in our minds they sometimes offer alternatives to believing and trusting in God. The problem with the following models is that they do not acknowledge God as an agent of change.

The first model is what I call the ***insight model*** or ***"figure it out" model***. This model was one of the first in our Western culture to develop and is based on the belief that insight leads to change. On the surface this sounds commendable. We read books or have conversations to gain insight, and some of this insight is inspirational for us. However, insight by itself is powerless.

Many people recognize that they have addictions. They see the horrible effects on their lives, but cannot stop. They have learned coping skills upon coping skills, but still cannot stop the addictive behavior. They have no real power behind their understanding of how to change.

Some read stacks of books and articles on building healthy relationships, but cannot manage to have healthy relationships. As mentors, it is easy to fall into this trap ourselves. We try to give advice to those we are counseling. We recommend books, DVDs, and classes. By themselves, these materials are empty. All of the knowledge gained may even lead to the additional obstacle of arrogance. A tool setting on the bench rather than in the hand of the carpenter is only a tool. Don't rely on the tools, rely on the Carpenter.

The *skills building model* or *behavioral model* is commonly used in our modern world. The methods based on this approach can be helpful, especially for young children, but have some serious limits. We have found that behavior can be changed without a change of heart or without a conscious effort. By using systems of reinforcement and behavior modification plans we can affect changes in actions, but the heart may still be sick. We have free will and I believe we can make choices contrary to the way we have been reinforced.

There is a story of a psychology class that decided to condition their professor to sit on his desk while he lectured. The students agreed to act distracted by dropping pencils, coughing, looking away, etc. each time he walked away from his desk. When he moved toward his desk they gave him eye contact and attended more closely to what he was saying. By the end of the lecture he was sitting on his desk while he spoke. Without his being aware of it, they had controlled his behavior.

We can do the same with our children, spouses and clients,

but there are limitations. God gave each of us a soul. It is an indescribable part of us that cannot be measured or conditioned by reinforcement. It is eternal and designed to commune with our Creator. It is something that secular psychologists find impossible to understand, and it is discounted by most. But this intangible soul is at the center of change and life and must be part of our efforts to help people.

The *humanistic model* or *freedom model* is probably the most commonly used. It is operated from the assumption that when a person is set free from the things in life that hinder or confine him, then he will become "good." It is believed that people are good at the core of their being and this goodness needs to be uncovered. This is, of course, very popular and gives us warm fuzzy feelings about ourselves.

We want to believe that we are good, but is that really true? Is a very young child who has just come into the world naturally giving, generous and kind to others? Or does he scream, hit and punch, insisting on his own way? I think God made children very small so they will not kill the rest of us to get their bottle or stuffed toy. Children need to be trained to be "good." Children who are not given boundaries and instruction are selfish and destructive to others. That is our nature. By nature we are children of wrath (Ephesians 2:3, NASB).

The more we rely on the goodness of people and abandon God's commands, the more we need prisons, medications and government control to keep peace. It is not our nature to be good. Therefore, models that are based on the notion that we are good will not work well.

The last model in the progression of psychology is the *solution focused model.* This examines what works in a person's life and what doesn't. This model offers solutions that supposedly already exist in the individual. It perpetuates the digging of dry wells. Jeremiah teaches about the futility of pursuing activities and dreams that lead to emptiness (Jeremiah 2:13). Lifetimes are spent digging dry wells when our God has already given us the Living Water. If the "solutions" are immoral and ultimately destructive to the person's eternal soul, a solution focused model sends him further down that road.

These are the models of the world. They do not allow God to be a part of the solution. However, a Spirit focused model is what I propose as the ideal. It is not based on figuring things out, changing only our behavior, humanistic choices, or seeking solutions from within ourselves. It is based on God making changes within our soul and Him setting the course for our lives. He will heal us if we let go of our human ambitions and plans.

Truth #2 - The Spirit is Gently and Tenaciously Seeking a Close Relationship with Every Person, No Exceptions.

The second truth of the spirit focused model is a big one: God is working in every person. The Holy Spirit is described by Jesus as The Helper. I see Him move in a gracious and gentle manner, never being dictatorial or intrusive. God's Spirit loves every human being way beyond his ability to imagine. He is working to soften everyone's heart and wants to have a close, personal relationship with every person, regardless of what he has done or how far away he might be from Him. He will nudge, softly speak, and arrange circumstances to give us another chance, but will not force us to listen; neither does He insist that we obey.

God is searching each person and working to soften him and direct him into fellowship with Him. This is His greatest and most earnest desire. I believe God is working in the heart of even the most hardened criminal who appears to be totally given over to evil. God is present wherever there is a sliver of space for Him to work.

I have performed suicide evaluations on men in detention facilities who have been arrested for serious violent crimes. I am very grateful to know that some of these men are locked up behind thick concrete walls for the rest of their lives. They have no detectable remorse for their crimes, no interest to live and no desire to nurture or love anyone else. In fact, they express intense hatred toward themselves, others and God. Some have no serious reservation about hurting or killing another person, including me.

But it is my belief that these men are not beyond the reach of God Almighty. He knows their hearts and can work in their lives to bring them closer to Him. He loves them in the same way that He loves us. This belief that God is drawing each person to Him is most important.

After the first few appointments with a person or couple, many peer counselors report that the case is impossible. The clients are too entrenched in the problem and although there may be hope, it is so small in comparison to the problem. These are the cases where God's Spirit is obviously at work. Nothing, or no one else, can be given credit when these people improve.

To be like God is to have a will to bring each person we meet closer to our Lord. Just as God's Spirit works to soften and bring each person closer, we are to work toward this goal, even if it seems impossible to us. We have hope when no one else does because we believe God is present and working.

Truth #3 - The Presence of God Changes People

This is a great mystery. God is so great that just to be near Him will make us better. As a counselor, I tend to over-think my role. It isn't complicated. If I can lead my client to spend time with God then my work is done. Jesus is always the answer. The process, the path, may look different each time, but every human being who needs help needs to spend time with the Helper. Sometimes my own lack of belief is revealed as I give advice and forget to lead a client toward a more authentic relationship with God. Remember, this is not the "figure it out model," it is about God and His presence. We often forget this great truth. We may acknowledge it at some level, but when we give advice and feel responsible to fix someone with our ideas, we are in essence taking over God's job and not truly believing that He can effect change in the person.

Many times in counseling appointments I have discussed with clients some truth about God. At the time, it doesn't really seem to mean anything to them. They may understand at an intellectual level, but it doesn't sink in. Later in the week they call and tell me of something exciting they just learned, as if they had never heard it before. It is the same thing we talked about in our appointment, but this time it was God who revealed it to them, so it seemed new and real. It is God's revelation that changes them. As humans, we talk a lot, but when God reveals something, it causes instant change.

Truth #4 - We are the Instruments of His Blessings

We are the hands, feet, and in this case, the ears of Jesus. When we listen, we are facilitating connections to God. At first we are the power cords from them to God. We have no power of our own, but God sends His love and power through us. If all has gone well in counseling they ultimately develop direct relations to God.

We are the tools the Carpenter uses to sculpt the wood. In the case of the apostle Paul, Jesus himself appeared to Paul on the road to Damascus, spoke to him and blinded him. This intervention was not made through other people. In my observation, this type of interaction is rare today. Many other Biblical accounts involve God sending and speaking through his servants. This is our role as peer counselors. God intervenes through us. It is humbling and difficult at times. I would not say He needs us to accomplish His will, but in His great wisdom, He chooses us to do His work.

Chapter 7
Spirit Focused Counseling: The ABC's

"Does not wisdom call out?
Does not understanding raise her voice?"

Proverbs 8:1

Acknowledge the struggle

Build Two Stories

Choose a path

Spirit Focused Counseling consists of "steps" which generally occur in sequence, but may be repeated. Counseling is never the same because no two people or couples are the same. This model can offer guidance and structure, but keep in mind that the goal is to love people, not fit them into a model.

At the end of each section in this chapter is a brief outline for quick reference and questions to ask clients. It is perfectly acceptable to bring this book into appointments for reference. My clients seem to appreciate my efforts to draw from other sources to help them.

Acknowledge the Struggle

If ten people looked out a window over the ocean and were asked to describe what they saw, you would get ten different descriptions. One individual might notice the wind driving the waves into the shore. Another might notice the different birds in the sky and describe their behavior. Someone else might point out the color of the water and sky and observe the light piercing through the clouds and reflecting off the water. There is so much to see in any given moment that we cannot pay attention to all of it, nor understand it and incorporate it all into our awareness. Therefore, we must be deliberate about what we pay attention to.

This same truth applies to counseling and mentoring. We can only pay attention to a portion of what is being said and let the rest pass away. This is the first step in counseling: being deliberate about what we are paying attention to. It begins when we *listen for the oppression they have experienced.* It is characteristic of humans that we must tell our story, and in doing so we are stronger. If we have a story inside that is not told, somehow it shrinks and morphs into something less real. But when we say the words, we are released from the power of it. It is freeing to tell a story about ourselves.

These stories are often unpleasant to hear. There are themes of violence, betrayal, loneliness and deep hurt. But we must hear these sad tales for the healing to begin. We not only must hear these stories, we must convey to the story tellers that we have heard them. Otherwise, they could tell their stories to trees and feel better. The healing aspect of telling about the oppression is knowing for certain that someone else understands or at least is intently trying to understand. This is called empathy - when we hear the story and can convey that we understand. This creates supernatural moments in time. God is always present when a hurting person is heard and is comforted.

Our goal as counselors and mentors is to love and work exactly as God does. When we do this, we *show supernatural empathy*. We must believe each person is loved by God and the Spirit desires to work with him in whatever way he will accept. The space where God is present may be only the size of a mustard seed, but I believe it is always there.

When we first hear the stories of some people, their faith to rely on God seems nonexistent and it appears hopeless that they can overcome their problems. They especially feel overwhelmed by their circumstances. If we are effectively listening and having empathy, we will feel the same way: hopeless and helpless. The first goal of counseling is to feel and think like they do. We jump in the deep and dirty pit with them by feeling what they feel. Once they sense we are with them in the pit, something amazing happens; God brings supernatural healing to the core of their being.

This is the beginning of our work. It is how the Holy Spirit uses us in a supernatural way. The selflessness that is required to arrive in the pit with them is only achieved by first experiencing God in our own lives. It is essential that we have felt God's hand lift us out of the pit. Our pit will not be the same as theirs, but we can empathize with their condition if we have been there and have been lifted out by the saving hand of God.

A nonbeliever can achieve a level of empathy with others, but not to the depth or accuracy of someone who has truly experienced God's supernatural empathy and healing when he has been broken and in his own pit. By being so blessed to have experienced God in this way, He gives us the power to do this for someone else, thus showing God to them. This is the deepest expression of love, and it will shake the foundations of a person. This is the beginning. It will spark a change in them that may grow into a small flame.

Listen for the two stories that co-exist in the same person. We will hear the oppressive story of fear, hopelessness, weakness, godlessness etc. The other story is one of courage, hope, faith and love. While the dark forces rage in their lives, the Holy Spirit is also there in power. This is why Christians can be so effective in helping people. We can tune our ears to listen for how God is alive in their stories. Be counter-intuitive to the problem and intuitive to the Spirit. I call this "Spiritual Intuition."

Example: Jack and Wendy came in for couples counseling. They brought their six month old infant with them. They had been married for two years and Wendy was not feeling love for Jack or for their baby, although she appeared to have the ability to care for the infant and keep him content during the appointment. She had maintained a relationship from before their marriage with a man who she described as a good friend who is more physically attractive than her husband. Although she spent long periods of time with this friend, she reported there was no physical contact. She had not pursued a marital relationship with this man because she felt he would not make a responsible husband. Jack had strong feelings of affection toward Wendy and the baby and was willing to do whatever was required to make their marriage work. They reported feeling best together, as a couple, when they were in church.

In this short snapshot, we first hear the story of a young family that has serious commitment problems, emotional infidelity, and possibly sexual adultery. There is much fear, doubt, and great potential for separation and emotional pain. This is obvious to everyone, especially the couple who is living it.

But we also hear the story of a family who, despite significant trouble, has reached out together to seek help and have made the effort to sit down with strangers to seek solutions to their problems. They are fighting against the problem to the degree they are still together and are cooperating in caring for their young son. Wendy is showing the ability to discern that her husband has better character than her friend, and Jack is willing to forgive her and move forward in the relationship. They also share and enjoy a spiritual connection with each other and actively spend time together seeking Christian fellowship and worshiping God at church. God is active in their lives by convicting them of their "sins" and has given them grace by providing an older Christian with whom to share. God has also blessed them with a healthy and content child through the miracle of conception and birth.

Two stories exist in the same couple, and both are absolutely true. The job of the counselor is to extract the ways they have succeeded and note how God is moving in their lives. He can also point out how they are participating in faith, with the Spirit, to fight against the problem. These victories always exist. Even if no victories can be noticed, the fact that the couple can even talk about the problem is a huge exception in and of itself. The people who are 100% overtaken by their problem cannot talk about it, or it may have overcome them to the degree they have taken their own lives through suicide. The fact that they are breathing and speaking is evidence there is a great deal of force working against the problem. We just have to notice it for them.

Listen for the sin that is the root of the problem. The root of every problem is sin. Either it is their sin or someone else's, but sin is the root. The only exception to this may be grieving. When someone is grieving the loss of someone, something or even grieving the loss of an idea or dream, then the root is a loss. For everyone else, sin is the problem. This is not a popular notion in our culture or even in our churches, but it is true and necessary to comprehend if we are to understand the struggle of others.

Sin takes many forms and shapes. When listening to someone's story, we will hear the struggles and oppression he has experienced. Because of the culture we live in, it is most likely understood in a context that is separate from God's

Kingdom. Problems will be referenced in terms of dysfunction, disorders, struggles and syndromes, but the word "sin" will most likely not be in his vocabulary when describing his situation.

For example, people may say they have a problem of overeating, or have a problem of eating too much comfort food. This, in truth, is a sin of gluttony. The mislabeling of the problem causes it to perpetuate itself. Freedom can only be obtained if the sin is identified, repented of and forgiven. Otherwise, dark forces are holding them captive and the power of the sin remains. "You shall know the truth and the truth shall make you free" (John 8:32). If they do not identify a sin as a sin then they cannot be set free from it. The root of the problem remains unless we remove it.

Traditional psychotherapy hamstrings clients by not addressing the root of the problem and instead calls the sin other terms that take the responsibility away from the person. This is a travesty and one reason to exercise caution when referring anyone to a secular counselor. Keep in mind that in the beginning stages of counseling it is not our job to point out sins, but to simply listen to how they understand and talk about their story. Later it will be possible to address the matter in ways they may accept, but initially we listen and remain quiet. We can only confront as much as we have supported, so at this point we need to spend time listening so that later we can have the rapport to bring up ideas to which they may otherwise take offense.

Clients will probably understand their problems in a context that makes them seem unsolvable to them. They may have accepted labels that render the problems permanent and/or made the problems their identity. This creates a dilemma because they cannot fight against themselves. Another issue may be that the clients do not put their lives or problems into a spiritual context. The struggle may not be understood from a spiritual perspective and thus the sin cannot be recognized.

Validate their experiences and appreciate the efforts they have waged against the problem. Validation is one of the most powerful tools that God has provided to help people. God designed us to connect with each other. We are made to experience life together, so when a person has an experience or a feeling that he cannot share with another person, it may seem "less real."

I worked in an outpatient mental health program where we held daily therapy groups for those who were diagnosed with Schizophrenia. For about one and a half hours we talked about whatever they wanted or needed to talk about. In one particular group, there were approximately 15 people in attendance. As the group concluded and everyone stood to leave the room, one male client hit another male client in the face! It was completely unprovoked and totally unexpected. The strange part was that the person who was hit acted as if he did not get hit, and the person who did the hitting acted as if he did not hit anyone. Everyone else in the room continued to exit as if nothing unusual happened. I saw it with my own eyes, but because of a lack of validation from others, I quickly began to doubt what I had just seen.

I stopped the two men as they were leaving the room and inquired about the event that had just occurred. The client who hit the man explained that he just had a sudden strong impulse to hit the other guy. I was, at this point, relieved to know that it did, in fact, happen. (It was unusual that so many individuals did not acknowledge the event, but this was due to their illnesses and medications.)

As human beings, we need someone else to experience life with us or we start to get a little crazy. Many times we just need to tell someone else what we see or what we experience emotionally to make us feel better and have a clearer perspective.

A young woman in her mid-twenties was attending coun-seling. She had a very low self-esteem and lived alone with her mother who was exceedingly controlling in every part of her daughter's life. Her mother had great expectations which she never could manage to meet. The mother had made the daughter very dependent on her and very unhappy. This young woman had set many goals for change, but could not accomplish any of them. It was just too hard.

One day while the woman was in the shower, she had a thought. "I always begin my shower by washing my left arm. What if I choose to begin with my right arm instead?" So she did, and it was earthshaking for her. Other actions up to that point were taken because her mother wanted her to, or they were reactions against her mother's wishes. This was one of the first actions she had taken on her own. She took power in a very small way, but it had an extreme effect. She and her counselor talked about this event and celebrated it! It was an amazing breakthrough - the beginning of purposeful and deliberate living. If this event had not been validated by the counselor the rest of the changes in her life may not have been possible.

Summary

Acknowledge the Struggle

- **Listen for the oppression they have experienced.**
- **Show supernatural empathy.**
- **Listen for the two stories that co-exist in the same person.**
- **Listen for the sin that is the root of the problem.**

- **Validate their experiences and appreciate the efforts they have waged against the problem.**

Sample Responses

- Can you see God working in your life?
- Tell me about your relationship with God.
- Do you ever feel God's presence?
- How has God kept you in the fight?
- Why haven't you given up?
- Why do you think God wants you here?
- How does God talk to people? How does God talk to you?

Build Two Stories

My first job after completing graduate school was to work with a group of men who were court-ordered to attend domestic violence counseling. Each of them had been violent with a wife or girlfriend and had gotten into some sort of trouble. Most were middle-aged and successful in their various professional fields.

We met as a group every week for two hours. This was the second and last phase of counseling for them. The focus of the first phase was to get them through their denial and to take responsibility for their actions. I facilitated a group designed to help them develop healthy boundaries and to deal with anger in an appropriate manner.

We started with approximately twelve men and it was a closed group, which meant that no new men could join once we began. We grew very close through the nine months that we met. During our last few meetings, we decided together to implement a "hot seat" session for each member of the group. This was a simple concept. Each week a different man would sit in the hot seat for two hours. The week prior, each of the other men would think and pray about this man's character then come back to the group with five positive character attributes and five items on which he needed to work. As we went around a semicircle, each man would share his character observations with the man on the hot seat until he understood each and every character quality that was pointed out. The man in the hot seat could not argue, discount, or defend himself. His only job was to understand others' perceptions of him.

Each member took a turn until everyone had spoken. Even though we never discussed prior to the group what feedback we were going to give, there were always undeniable themes that came out. It was tense and very emotional for us all. It was done in love, but there were some hurt feelings every week. I think of Proverbs 27:6: "Wounds from a friend can be trusted, but an enemy multiplies kisses." In a way, we wounded each other, but it was for the growth of our character. The wounds were from those we trusted.

Without exception, the men knew their character flaws. Feedback about their negative qualities was not new to them and they generally took it in stride without much display of emotion. However, when the positive character qualities were discussed, it was more difficult for them. They tried to minimize and deny them, but when everyone repeated the same things about them, the denial broke, and many wept. Each man had been told all of his life that he was a horrible person by his parents and others. They knew the negative qualities and had incorporated them into their identities then acted accordingly. The good in them was not recognized. It was foreign to them. The victories in their lives happened with no applause. I even took my turn in the hot seat and they let me have it with the good and the bad. It was hard to hear, but was life changing.

To begin the process of building two stories *ask them how they see God working in their lives*. Stay curious about your clients' stories and listen for their views about God. They may not see any spiritual strength in themselves, but can easily see the strength of the problem. Like the men in the story above, God's hand and the "good" may be hidden from them.

Invite them to see that they have faith and see how God is working in their lives. This is the step in counseling in which their faith and the power of God within them is brought to life. Once **you** have noticed the two stories in the person or in the couple, your next task is to invite **them** to see how God is working, and to show them their faith and strength against the problem. This is the hardest part of the whole process. A person may be blind to these things and can refute them much more easily than he can accept them. Many times, the space made for the problem in one's life far exceeds the space he has allowed for God and for his faith. This step is simply showing him the other side.

My three sons and I love to mountain bike on the trails in Western Colorado. Along the trails are numerous obstacles and dangers. I instruct my sons not to look at the obstacles they are trying to avoid or the drop-off to the side. I tell them, "Where you look, is where the rest of you will go." Your eyes turn, which turns your head, which turns your shoulders, which turns your arms, which steers your bike off the trail exactly where you are looking. If you want to look over the cliff, stop and enjoy the view, then continue to ride. Rather than focusing on an obstacle you wish to avoid, focus on the line through the obstacle, then you will make it through.

This same principle is true in life. Where we focus our attention is where we will soon be going. We want people to see God's hand in their lives so they will move toward Him. If they continue to talk and live in the problem, they will give the problem more power.

Someone who holds resentment or un-forgiveness toward another person will become like that person. The hate keeps him looking toward the negative qualities, or looking at what went wrong in the relationship and that is what is reinforced. I have seen people hold strong negative feelings towards others, which makes them develop the same negative qualities in themselves. Or it may bring to their attention others with the same negative qualities, which will increase the likelihood they will get involved in relationships with them. This is why God's power must be the center of discussion and focus.

Share the other story that you see. I do this by saying something like, "Would you be interested to hear how I see your story?" If they accept your input, carefully describe how they are persistent, how God must love them because they are still here and fighting, and discuss their qualities of tenacity and love for others. Positive qualities will become abundantly clear to you if you spend ample time listening and have spiritual intuition.

Stay behind as you help them see their strengths. This is a critical concept to understand. It is, however, one of the more difficult concepts to adopt as a counselor or mentor. Rather than giving advice and showing them the way, it is much more effective to let them discover the path away from their problems. Often, we may easily see the answers for them, but we must restrain our impulses to lead from the front. Pulling them along is tiring and can lead to frustration on our part. If they follow our advice, they may become dependent on us rather than on God. We see what needs to be done and naturally want to fix it, and fix it fast. If we simply tell them the way to go, we rob them of the chance to grow by discovering for themselves the direction God wants for them. We might see the way, but we have to hold back so they can learn to hear God's voice and discover His purpose.

Our ultimate goal is achieved when a couple or individual no longer needs us. We must consider their highest good. The problems they have when they walk in the door are most likely symptoms of not being connected with God. So our purpose is not to solve problems for them, but to show them how to find God in every situation. This is much harder than it may seem. The stories they tell and the struggles they have are interesting so it is tempting to get mixed up in trying to solve them. This can provide a test of our own motives. We must be sure we are in a relationship to help them rather than help ourselves. If we are directing their lives from the front we are not considering their deeper needs and are most likely attempting to satisfy our own need to help or rescue someone.

Once you have seen God in their lives and they have seen Him too, then God must be accepted and absorbed. They must redefine themselves in the light of these experiences. Even mature Christians who have healthy relationships with God still need others to help them through difficulties and help them see where God is working. Regardless of spiritual maturity level, everyone needs to occasionally reevaluate his view of God and his view of himself. We need to become aware of the sin in our lives, confess it and experience God's peace anew.

For many, this may be the first time someone has seriously listened to them in a spiritual context. They may have never had an example to follow and may be completely unfamiliar with trusting and listening to God. It is easy to take for granted our familiarity with prayer and communication with God. When I pray at the end of each session, I like to ask specifically how I can pray for them. I need to remember that this may be the first time anyone has ever prayed for them. It can be a powerful moment.

The whole purpose for this step is to have them accept God in their lives. I don't mean accept Jesus as their Savior, but accept and embrace that God is active and moving in every part of their lives. I fear that many have accepted Jesus as their Lord and Savior, but have not allowed Him to be pervasive and meaningful in every part and every cell of their beings. I believe many Christians leave worship service and immediately forget to bring God along to the rest of their lives. He is involved in our sin, in our failures, and in our successes. Monday morning He is there to live through the day with us.

When the person you are helping can reach out and take hold of God, you have finished this step of counseling. When he sees that God is relevant in his life and is a central part of any problem he may experience, then you are ready to move on. However, you may need to slide back to this point from time to time because we all need to be reminded that God is concerned and powerful to help in every circumstance. In Exodus 14:14 Moses said, "The Lord will fight for you, you need only to be still."

Do not let victories go by without applause. I heard of a therapist who would literally fall back in his chair in exuberance if a client did something wonderful that no one noticed. When he marked an un-noticed victory in this way, his clients would not forget that they had overcome something at that moment.

Please remember that this process may take time. It will most likely happen over a period of many appointments or conversations. They will update you on their circumstances and you may need to return to the first step of listening and accepting their struggle. Over time, they see the other side. They see the hope, the presence of God, the other life that is possible. Once they get a glimmer of hope, they are ready to consider a change.

Invite them to make these works of God and faith a part of their <u>redefinition</u>. Point out the ways they have overcome a problem to give meaning to life. Define the person not by the problem, but by what the Spirit is doing. So many people have come to me with lists of diagnoses that define them: "I am Obsessive Compulsive, ADHD and am a perfectionist." These defining labels may be placed on them by professionals or even themselves. In the absence of purpose and identity, even negative definitions of themselves is somehow soothing. This is indicative of living and accepting a life away from God. We all do this to some degree.

We need to reframe ourselves and our lives in the context of God's story of us. How does He see us? What is right and wrong in His eyes? What is His purpose in our lives? One of my most favored questions is, "If someone gave you ten million dollars to make the world a better place, and you cannot spend it on yourself, what would you do with the money?" I am amazed at the blank stares I get from people. Many really have no idea how to make the world better, and thus have no idea what their purpose is in life. I have noticed that people who know their talents and purpose answer that question with endless ideas for ministries and initiatives to help people, the environment, etc.

The key to assisting someone to a Godly definition is to help him slowly, over time, have conversation and thought about his personal issues and learn how his experiences are part of God's plan to fulfill a divine purpose. It comes alive when it becomes personal. It is as if he is a Biblical character and the story is written about him. When a person's meaning of life or point of reference is a spiritual one, then he experiences real healing and change. He is not coping, not just getting by, but living by the direction and conviction of the Holy Spirit and making that his story.

Summary

Build Two Stories

- **Ask them how they see God working in their lives.**
- **Invite them to see that they have faith and see how God is working in their lives.**
- **Share the other story that you see.**
- **Stay behind as you help them see their strengths.**

- **Invite them to make these works of God and faith a part of their <u>redefinition</u>.**

Sample Responses

- In light of the strength of the problem and its dominance in your life, how can you explain the existence of a force that opposes it? It should not be alive at all.

- Have there been times when God was directing you, but you did not notice?

- What does it say about your faith that it can survive in the atmosphere that it does?

- If your faith can survive without you noticing, what might happen if you paid attention to it and gave it the energy that has been historically given to the problem?

- What prevents the problem from getting worse?

- Doesn't it seem strange that the problem hasn't completely overcome you?

- Where did your faith come from?

- How can you explain the areas in your life that the problem hasn't been able to affect?

- What do you think God is doing about it? (The problem.)

- What prevents you from seeing God's hand in your life?

- I am amazed at you. How have you kept the problem at bay for so long?

- How can you use this talent even more?

- How can you make more space for God in your life and less space for the problem?

- Do you see the path that leads you away from the problem?

- If your faith continues to grow, what might people see?

- If Hollywood producers made a movie of your life, what would you give for the title?

- If you were a Bible character, how would your story progress?

- If you were to notice God's hand in your life more often, how would that change you?

- If you were more sure of your purpose for life, how would that change you?

- If God gave you power to do anything, what would you do?

- What do the angels in Heaven do when they see your faith?

Choose a Path

Formulate an attack plan against the problem. Once a client feels understood, can see the Spirit working and has made Him part of his identity, then an attack plan is formulated. Analyze the support system of the problem and discuss ways the Spirit may be moving against it. Wonder how he can increase resources for the attack.

Let go and Let **_God_** *do the work*. Remember it is their life to live and it is not yours. They are choosing a path and it is a choice that is only theirs to make. I encourage you to pray for others, especially if you find yourself thinking or worrying about them. Lift them up to God and let go. He can handle the burden. They may see God and choose not to follow. This is a perplexing situation, but I have seen it many times, sometimes to various degrees even within myself. A comforting thought is that we cannot see the end of the story; we see only a small part in the middle. God sees it all and my prayer, even for people who appear to reject truth and God's plan, is that someday they will make a decision to follow Him more closely.

Expect backward steps. Part of letting go is accepting that clients will take backward steps. Very few people pull out of a nose dive without some instability and veering to the left and right. Be an encourager and be supportive. When your clients are discouraged you can mark even slight changes. This can be extremely helpful. They will most likely be unable to see small changes, but we can point them out.

One method to keep people encouraged is to ***collapse time***. This can be done by seeing for them the changes they have made over a period of time. When change is slow it can be undetected. I might say, "Think of your life just one year ago and the thoughts/feelings you were experiencing. How do you see yourself now?" This is collapsing time backward. You may also help them collapse time forward by saying, "If you continue to change at this same steady pace, what could your life be like one year from now?"

Summary

Choose a Path

- **Formulate an attack plan against the problem.**
- **Let go and Let <u>God</u> do the work.**
- **Expect backward steps.**
- **Collapse time.**

Sample Responses:

- What are you doing that allows the problem to thrive?

- Who or what is helping the problem stay alive?

- Who could you enlist to help you?

- If the problem was suddenly gone, what would happen? (Possible response: "I wouldn't have anything to do.")

- Who would resist your efforts if you tried to change?

- Who would be affected if you changed?

- Who could help you in your struggle?

- If you continue to change at this same steady pace, what might your life be like one year from now?

- Think of your life just one year ago and the thoughts/feelings you were experiencing. How are you different now?

- Does the problem have a weak point, maybe an area that will not resist too strongly?

- Do you know someone who has successfully overcome the same kind of problem?

- What might you expect the problem/dark side to do once it realizes it is under attack?

Chapter 8
Miscellaneous Helpful Things

This chapter includes some of the things that have been most helpful to peer counselors over the years. They are from training sessions and from peer counselors themselves. Be creative, use them as they benefit you and let God develop your skills, tools and style. Your style will differ from all others, and that is an admirable thing.

Stories and Analogies

People absorb information in many different ways. As we counsel, we can sometimes simply state information while clients listen and comprehend. Many times, however, they can't hear through the usual direct methods. Strong emotions, stubbornness, resistance and a myriad of other factors can make it impossible to pass on even the simplest of information. Therefore, using a less direct approach like stories and analogies can be helpful.

Jesus was a master teacher and counselor. He knew his followers would not always absorb his teachings from a straight forward approach. But they could not resist hearing stories and, as he told them, the truths would slowly penetrate and simmer inside them. People are naturally attracted to stories. Our curiosity gets the best of us and we can be taught a great many things without even realizing it is happening. This back door approach is an enjoyable way to teach, and it is very effective.

Many people to whom we speak are not necessarily church-goers and some have had negative experiences in church. If we pull out the Bible, turn to a chapter and verse and then begin reading, we may lose them. Many people are closed to this teaching method because they have been spiritually beat up and judged by others who have pulled out the Bible, so when you quote scripture, they immediately put you in the same category and tune you out.

The same teaching can be achieved through more accept-able means. When I think a particular Bible story may be helpful, I simply begin telling the story without relating the source. I don't tell the story verbatim as it appears in scripture, but I make sure the truth that is taught from the story is accurate. They receive the teaching, the Spirit begins working through the truth, and they do not resist.

Children, especially, learn through stories. Their intel-lectual abilities to grasp a topic might be limited, but they love stories and can remember them for a lifetime. The truth in a story will stay with them, even if not at a conscious level.

Analogies are comparisons between two things that are similar in some way and are often used to explain something or make it easier to understand. They are parallel stories that offer another back door approach to teaching.

The Storm Analogy

When couples seek help with their relationships, it is usually after a fight, a prolonged conflict, or even after an affair has been discovered. Real damage has occurred to the relationship, and they are motivated by fear and pain to eliminate the source of the anguish. Sometimes they even want to eliminate each other. They come in attacking, blaming and refusing to work together. The storm analogy has been useful in getting couples to stop fighting, start the healing process, and ultimately to work together on rebuilding the relationships.

Everyone has personal experience with storms. We know, for example, that thunderstorms can be scary and can create damage. We also know that every storm ends and the sun eventually returns. We know very deep in our souls that storms come and go. They are part of the cycle of nature and we have a good idea what to expect.

On the other hand, our problems seem hopeless. It seems that they never end and we do not know what to expect. We have no idea where our problems may lead us and we are clueless on what actions to take. As counselors, if we can link storms and problems in our clients' minds, we successfully bestow understanding. If we can successfully link marital conflict with a storm, we can instantly teach that the trouble will not last forever and the sun will again come out in the relationship. This provides instant hope to hurting and confused people, and that is truly miraculous.

Step One - Damage Control If you have ever been on a boat during a storm at sea, you know it can be terrifying and perilous. The boat can be damaged or even sunk, people can fall overboard, and lives can be lost. During a severe storm, it is not the time to make repairs or to set sail to a destination. Damage control is the one and only goal when the storm is in full force. Keeping everyone safe and alive on the boat is the very best you can do. Don't attack your fellow crewmates, you might need them later. Don't try to set sail or make repairs or you may be washed overboard. Just stay calm and weather the power of the storm.

The same is true for a marriage that is in the center of a storm. Damage control should be the only goal. It's not the time to start solving lifetime problems or to set long term goals for the relationship. The energy should be focused on survival; just prevent further damage and keep the family intact. Do not bring children into the arguments and do not set them against the other spouse. Do not use hurtful language or violence. Do not turn to drugs and alcohol or escape into other addictive behaviors. Do not have an affair. Do not do things to "get even" with the other person. Many couples mistakenly want to start repairs before they are ready or able. It is a relief to them to have a simplified goal of not making it worse. I like to ask the question, "What would you do to make all of this worse?" They are usually shocked at this question, but can easily answer it. This question defines and delineates what they shouldn't do. This is their damage control. They must eventually move into the repair phase but can only do so once the storm begins to subside.

Unfortunately, some couples cannot refrain from harming each other or their children emotionally and/or physically. Damage control in their situations is not successful. In these instances, a limited time of physical separation for the purpose of prayer and reflection may be the best course to take. This must be done very cautiously, with specific goals in place, because some couples never come back together to attempt to work things out.

Step Two - Making Repairs After the couple has achieved relative success in the damage control phase, they can progress to making repairs. The storm has calmed and there is less threat of danger to the crew, so repairs to the ship may begin. During the repairs, however, the storm may once more rise up and damage control may again be necessary for a time.

During reconstruction, confessions and apologies may be made, forgiveness extended, and love rekindled. At this point, absence of conflict is not the goal. Rather, productive conflict is necessary. Some issues can only surface in anger or when someone is upset. These issues are pushed out into the open and may be ugly and painful but absolutely necessary to confront for true healing to occur. Before moving to the next step of sailing, be sure the crew is rested and ready for the work ahead. Give permission to relax and take time for healing.

Step Three - Setting Sail Every person, couple and family has divine work to do in this life. It is not necessarily the work we do for money or our careers, although it could be. It is the work God purposed for us to do for His glory and His Kingdom. For this work, He has given everyone gifts to utilize. It is our life purpose to discover these gifts and use them for Him. If people are not searching for or attempting to fulfill their divine purposes, they will become distracted and fall back into turmoil. Ships are safe in the harbor, but that is not what they are built for. We are all designed to work in His Kingdom, although it may at times be laborious. Once the repairs are made on the ship, then we can set sail on our divine adventure. It cannot be done during a great storm or on a ship that is damaged, but when the conditions are right the ship is ready to set sail.

Empty Wells Analogy

> "My people have committed two sins: they have forsaken me, the spring of living water, and have dug their own cisterns, broken cisterns that cannot hold water" (Jeremiah 2:13).

A useful counseling analogy can be found in this scripture. Many people find themselves spending their lives on things that ultimately are not useful to God. In Jeremiah, Israel had once again turned from God and was worshiping idols rather than seeking and following God. They rebelled against God's springs of living water and dug their own dry wells. Some people dig one great big well over the course of their lives. They pour their efforts into a single area of futility: fortune, fame, career, etc. Even noble causes like raising children or doing church work can become idols - more important than our relationship with God.

While some have wasted lifetimes seeking a single idol of their heart, others may seek many different idols. They move from one area to another digging multiple wells that do not hold water rather than accept God's living water. A line of questions can be used in this analogy to help people see their errant courses: "What empty wells have you dug in your life?" "What wells have your family dug with your assistance?" "What are you searching for that you believe God cannot provide?" "What has been the cost of digging these wells?" "What does God think of your wells?"

Sometimes people already have their own analogies. Scripture uses many types of analogies as well: farming, spiritual warfare, searching for lost things, vines and branches, and many others. Some counselors choose not to use stories and analogies. Use what works for you.

Character

All my clients have character flaws. I am not immune from these shortcomings and neither are you. We sometimes strive too hard to solve problems and not work hard enough to develop stronger character. I have heard it said, "God is more interested in developing your character than in fixing your circumstances." I believe this is true and I have observed that difficult circumstances are generally caused by our character flaws. It is the spiritual law of sowing and reaping.

God will not save us repeatedly from the consequences of our sin and bad judgment. He wants us to learn and grow. In fact, I have witnessed, time after time, that life's lessons are repeated until learned. Clients come to me with assorted problems over an extended period of time and they cannot perceive that there is a theme running through all of their experiences and stories. These problems result from character flaws that produce consequences in all parts of their lives. Unwanted consequences will persist until the character is changed. God may allow us many opportunities to grow by presenting these lessons repeatedly in various ways and by various circumstances.

Humans are stubborn and often completely blind to their character deficiencies. As peer counselors, we can assist our clients to notice their deficiencies and use them to grow in Godly character. This may be our greatest gift to them, but it is not an easy task. Some peer counselors are gifted with the ability to discern a person's character and know how to proceed. This is a great blessing. For these gifted counselors and especially for the rest of us, I recommend a book regarding character.

The Power for True Success: How to Build Character in Your Life[1] is an exceptional book that I use as a spirit-based diagnostic and treatment tool. It lists 49 character qualities with scriptures, photos and quotes to help us grow in these qualities. When I am working with someone and cannot pinpoint the root problem, this book helps to identify the flaw in their character. Because this book compares one's character to that of Jesus, it is also an exceptional family devotional book.

Drama Triangle

This is an excellent tool for conceptualizing dysfunctional relationships. It was first described by Stephen Karpman in 1968 and is a method you can use to discover and define the sinful and sick behaviors within relationships. Participation in this Drama Triangle keeps people disconnected from Godly relationships and holds them in bondage of blame, guilt, shame, and unforgiveness. The relationships defined in the triangle are not perpetuated at a real, conscious level. Instead, these behaviors are reactions to others and were most likely learned from families.

Rescuer   Persecutor

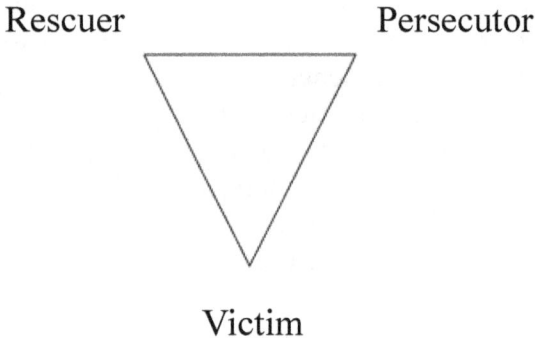

Victim

Each of the corners of the triangle represents a dysfunctional role a person may assume. It takes at least two people to play in this triangle, but there may be dozens involved, even people who are no longer living.

Many people come to counseling playing the role of **victim**. They see themselves as helpless against outside forces and people who are playing the role of persecutor. Their behaviors are based on fear, and they allow things to occur so that they will feel safe and can avoid responsibility. They expect others to meet their needs and hold resentment when their needs are unmet.

The **persecutor** behaves in a reactionary manner as well and controls others as a way to feel safe. He deals with stress or new ideas with criticism, blame and even physical attacks. He must be in control at all costs to avoid responsibility and fear. Persecutors are often self-righteous and judgmental.

The **rescuer** uses dominance, as well, to feel safe and to avoid his own problems. He sees himself as morally superior and must help others in order to feel good. Rescuers gravitate toward caretaker roles and often feel underappreciated and resentful toward others.

To illustrate this, a couple recently came to me for marital counseling. The purpose of counseling was to help Debbie, who was feeling overwhelmed and depressed. Her husband, Mike, made the appointment without her knowledge. Mike was the rescuer at this point, but moved into the persecutor role when he immediately described his wife as lazy and weak. Debbie quickly assumed the victim role and began crying at his criticisms. Mike, of course, became angry and expected me to "fix" her. He wanted me to play into the Drama Triangle as the rescuer. Debbie continued to cry and invited me to play the rescuer by dramatically yelling, "Tell me what I'm supposed to do, he's driving me crazy!"

These types of relationships are common. The Drama Triangle can help you get a better picture of what is happening and how to intervene or, in some cases, how not to intervene. This is only a very brief overview. If you find this model helpful, more information is available online, in articles and in books.

Confronting Sin

A common question among peer counselors and mentors is how to confront sin in a person's life. We often observe that sin is causing negative repercussions, but do not want to drive the person away by bringing up the problem. The rule to follow is to **confront as much as you have supported.** The time you spend listening and showing empathy can be compared to money placed into an account. Over time it builds and can be spent. If you confront more than you have supported, then the account is overdrawn and the person disconnects from you. If you approach random people on the street to tell them they are sinning and need to repent, they may completely discount you. Confronting clients before you have supported them has the same effect. However, if you confront a long time friend, it will deeply affect him. It is the trust and the time that you're leveraging.

It is not uncommon for clients to come for relationship counseling, but they are not married and may have children together. Some have even lied to us and said they are married, but reveal later they are living together. To say nothing may lead them to believe there is no problem with this. To make judgmental statements will most likely drive them away from a potential spiritually healing relationship with their mentors. Statements like, "We don't judge you for this decision, but we do want you to know that we believe by living together you may be missing a special blessing God has for married couples." I also may explain that God has a plan for sexual relationships and families and by living together they may be "outside of God's protection." These are ways to softly confront the sin but stay in loving connection with the sinners. It is God's job to do the convicting.

"Instead, speaking the truth in love, we will grow to become, in every respect, the mature body of Him who is the head, that is, Christ" (Ephesians 4:15).

Emotional Funnel

We all have many feelings. Some are unpleasant so we try to avoid them if possible. We might even feel the "wrong" feeling. For example, on a construction site, a young man may make a mistake and cut a board wrong. On the surface he will most likely show anger, especially if others are watching. The feeling of anger is socially acceptable in that setting. The true feelings may be embarrassment and inadequacy, but they are not expressed. Instead, they are funneled into anger.

This can happen repeatedly until the true feelings are not recognized or properly released and a build-up of emotion occurs. I often ask the question, "What is behind the anger?" or "What is behind the depression?" Anger and depression are legitimate feelings, but they can cover up and bury other feelings. This can be illustrated by "The Male Emotional Funnel System" from a book entitled Men Who Batter.

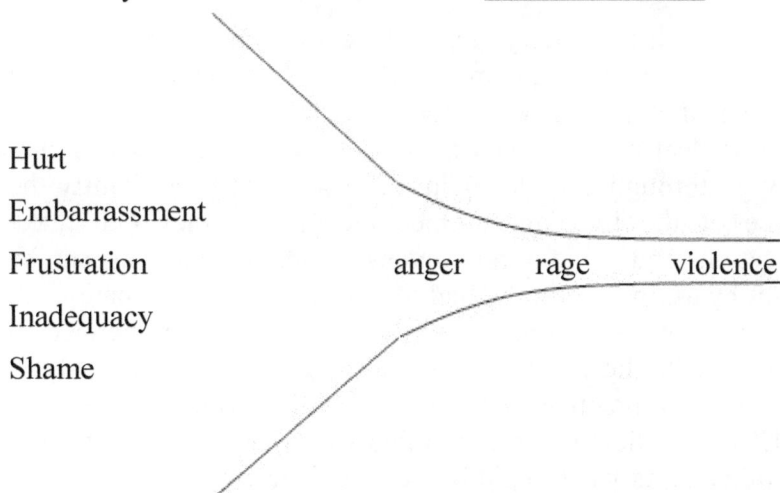

Hurt

Embarrassment

Frustration   anger   rage   violence

Inadequacy

Shame

I draw this diagram often to provide a visual picture of what may be occurring. It helps people reach and understand their actual deeper feelings, thus assisting in the healing process. This concept is not limited to men. Everyone will misidentify feelings by changing them into emotions that are more socially acceptable to express.

HALT

Frequently, people have trouble recognizing when they are getting overloaded. Before they realize it, they are overwhelmed and don't know how they got to that point. HALT is an acronym to help identify the source of the problem before it grows into a bigger problem.

Hungry

Angry

Lonely

Tired

Being a little hungry, angry, lonely or tired is fine, but in extremes it can cause an emotional wreck. This acronym is used as a mental stop sign. When they start feeling uneasy, or notice that they feel out of balance, the word HALT comes to mind. They go through each letter in the word HALT to identify the source of the imbalance. Once recognized, they can make corrections and avoid a more intense problem later. This can be taught by asking the individual to stop and analyze situations in the recent past where he felt out of control or overwhelmed. It helps to write the word on a board or paper so they get a visual picture. They practice this with you until eventually the word HALT automatically comes to mind whenever they need to stop and think about what might be causing their imbalance.

Prayer

Many who request counseling as new or immature Christians have little experience with prayer. When teaching people to pray, I have found that writing down the acronym ACTS is beneficial. It provides an outline from which to start.

Adoration to God

Confession to God

Thanksgiving

Supplication

It is recommended that you assist others in praying by modeling this. Before praying, write down an outline with items under each of these four letters.

Genograms

I find genograms to be invaluable. They provide a method to record a great deal of information in a small space. A genogram is similar to a drawing of a family tree. It displays names, ages, and relationships of family members, but also can tell stories and show hidden family patterns. With modern families often blended from other family groups - divorce, remarriage, children in the home from past relationships - it all gets jumbled. I easily forget people's names and their relationships to everyone else in the family so this affords a way to remember those important details.

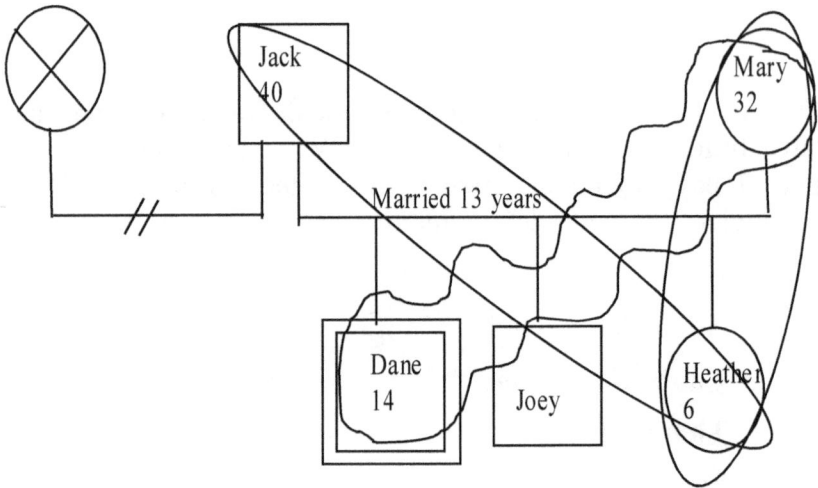

A genogram uses symbols to organize information. For example, in this simple genogram I can determine that this family consists of a mother, a father and three children. The father was previously married, had no children, and his first wife is deceased. There is strife between the mother and the oldest son, but the relationship between the youngest child, a female, and both parents is strong. Also note that the age of the oldest son indicates he was born before the couple married and, with some math, you can figure out that Mary was 18 when this child was born. A double box around the oldest son indicates he is the "identified patient" and the reason the family is requesting counseling.

As you can see, this is a powerful tool. I have invented additional symbols and I write notes all over my genograms to record even more information. The clients love it as well, and feel important when you take the time to record their family information accurately. This can be used not only to gather and record information, but also to make predictions and analyze relationships within the family.

For example, with this genogram I can speculate that Joey feels left out of the family. With the strong bond to Heather and conflict focused on Dane, he may feel ignored and may possibly act-out soon. The mother may hold guilt over her unwed pregnancy that occurred at an early age that may have pushed the couple into marriage. There are many books and online information available if you decide to use this tool.

Questions

"It is better to know some of the questions than all of the answers."

James Thurber

Questions can do the work of countless hours of lecture. They are the backdoor approach to getting information into someone's head and heart. Be careful to ask questions only after you have developed a relationship through listening. Questions can give the person direction, and we must be careful anytime we are providing direction for an individual. Some questions are difficult to answer so if your client is struggling to respond or giving you superficial answers, you may want to give the question as a homework assignment. The following questions are in categories, but please do not be limited to these questions. Develop your own as well. Be curious, carefully listen to the responses, and never assume you know how someone will answer.

Direction Questions

Beginning of Session

- What dreams do you have for your future?
- a) If you were given 3 million dollars to change the world for the better, and could not spend it on yourself, what would you do with the money?

   b) In that same theme, with the resources you currently have, what is one small thing you can do today toward your cause?
- What is it that you want to talk about?
- What do you need, that you do not have?
- When you are at the end of your life looking back, what would you want to see as your greatest success?

Middle of Session

- Out of everything that we have talked about, what is the most important thing to work on?
- What themes do you see running through the topics we talked about?
- What is helpful about our time together?
- What do you like about the path that you are currently on?

End of Session

- What will your life look like when you do not need counseling anymore?
- Even though there are things in your life that are not the way you want them to be, do you believe you can move forward in other areas?

Goal Questions

- How can you increase your strength in your life to make the right decisions?
- What lessons have been repeated in your life that you have not learned from?
- How could you rephrase that goal so it depends only on what you do and not on what others do?

Going Deeper Questions

- Is there something that we have not talked about that we should discuss?
- What do you care the most about?
- At what time in your life did you feel most alive?
- What has been the high point of your life so far?
- What is an event that shaped you as a person?
- a) Name a person who has significantly impacted your life for the good.

  b) How are you similar to him/her? How are you different?

God Questions

- Where is God in all of this?
- How does God talk to you?
- What character quality is God working on you to change?
- What things in your life do you think God is pleased with?
- What has been the most important spiritual experience in your life?
- a) What things have people complemented you about?

  b) What spiritual gifts do you think these are?

  c) Do you feel led to use these gifts more?
- What do you like the most about God?
- What do you dislike about God?

Confronting and Responsibility Questions

- What things do you do that make your problems worse?
- a) On a scale from 1 to 10, how likely is it that you will (state whatever goal they may have)?

  b) Are there any obstacles we need to address to make this more possible?
- What negative fruit do you see in your life?
- a) What part of this situation is under your control, and what is not?

  b) What can you do to change your part?

  c) What about the part you cannot change?

- a) What short-term goals can you realistically make at this time without becoming overwhelmed?

  b) What is a healthy amount of activity?

- a) What did you do well in this situation?

  b) What can you do better next time?

- What decisions have you made in your life that caused some of the problems you now experience?

Motivation Questions

- What are you most passionate about in life?

- What are the things you do in life that give you the greatest amount of energy?

- What things are most disturbing to you?

- a) On a scale of 1 to 100, how committed are you to your spouse?

  b) (Suppose they said 20.) If you had the motivation, what would you do to move from a 20 to a 21?

- a) What are you willing to sacrifice in order to accomplish this goal?

  b) Is there anything you would not do to accomplish this goal?

- What would your life be like if you never worked on this problem?

- What is the cost of not pursuing your dream (or working on the problem)?

Repentance Questions

- Do you think God can forgive you for this?

- a) In what ways have you already tried to overcome your problem?

  b) What was the impact?

- a) What has been damaged in your life because of this sin?

  b) Can God bring this back to life?

- If a genie appeared and offered to change anything about yourself, what would it be?

- a) Are there any lies that you believe about yourself?

  b) Are there any lies about you that you believed in the past but no longer believe?

Questions for Couples

Allow both husband and wife

to answer each question.

- What needs to be different in your relationship?
- What does God need to do in your relationship?
- What can the husband do to love his wife more?
- What can the wife do to respect her husband more?
- How is your relationship with God?
- How can we pray for you this next week?

Seminars

I have attended many seminars over the years but these two score a "10" on a scale of 1-10. I do not agree with 100% of the material presented, but these seminars will help you to grow considerably as Christians and as peer counselors.

Peacemakers Ministries is an amazing organization that offers workshops throughout the United States on Biblical conflict resolution. I have been blessed by attending the seminar and reading <u>The Peacemaker</u> by Ken Sande.

Go to www.peacemaker.net for more information.

The Basic Youth Conflicts Seminar presented by the Institute in Basic Life Principles definitely changed my life and the lives of those around me. The seminar is not only for youth, but for everyone. You will grow spiritually from the wisdom gained from this material.

More information is available at www.iblp.org.

Belief Tree

This paradigm can be utilized by peer counselors to detect the roots of various issues, then discover ways to overcome them. The tree model begins by examining the "bad fruit" in a person's life. The "bad fruit" may manifest as difficulties in relationships, bad behavior, mean words, etc., but is only a product of deeper things. Some clients are visually oriented and may find this or similar diagrams helpful.

Fruit– Wrong actions, words and behaviors

Branches– Wrong Choices

Trunk– The things that are important to us.

What we want in life.

Roots– Belief system (False Beliefs)

False Beliefs Toward Myself	False Beliefs Toward Others	False Beliefs Toward God
Curses, lies, false identities	Judgments, unholy vows, hurts and wounds	Wrong idea of who God is and what He is like

Scripture

The last and most powerful "helpful thing" is our Father's Holy Word. The practice of scripture memorization is rare and, I fear, growing more so every passing day. I like to recommend that my clients write down scriptures and commit them to memory, or at least post select scripture on their refrigerators, cell phones, computer screens, or other frequently seen places. The power to change comes from knowing the truth and engrafting it into our hearts and minds. My recommendations are not always followed, but I have witnessed the power of God change people to the core when they read and memorize scripture.

Chapter 9
The Calling

"When we choose to follow God beyond where our own strengths can take us, He rescues us from our small prisons of triviality and fear-and this is a good and beautiful and freeing thing."

Marvin Olasky in <u>World Magazine</u>*, Dec. 2008*

God's Instructions for Us

The idea of performing counseling or encouraging someone in distress is intimidating for most people. We do not believe we have the wisdom to help others and fear that we won't have the answers that those in need have come to find. We are afraid that we will sit there speechless. We tell ourselves that we don't have our lives completely together, so how can we help others? These ideas are very common, but can be overcome. Part of the journey to believe in your ability to perform counseling is to see what counseling or mentoring really is. In order to demystify counseling, allow me to break the counseling relationship into some basic parts. I can do this by looking at the "one another" passages in the New Testament. These verses instruct us how to relate to each other in a Godly manner. These will be quoted from the New American Standard Bible.

Romans 12:10 "Be devoted to one another in brotherly love; give preference to one another in honor."

Romans 12:16 "Be of the same mind toward one another…"

Romans 13:8 "...love one another..."

Romans 14:13 "Therefore let us not judge one another..."

Romans 14:19 "…pursue the things which make for peace and the building up of one another."

Romans 15:5 "…be of the same mind with one another according to Christ Jesus."

Romans 15:7 "…accept one another..."

Romans 15:14 "…admonish one another."

1 Corinthians 12:25 "so that there may be no division in the body, but that the members may have the same care for one another."

Galatians 5:13 "...serve one another."

Galatians 6:2 "Bear one another's burdens…"

Ephesians 4:1-2 "….forbearing one another in love." (ASV)

Ephesians 4:32 "Be kind to one another, tender-hearted, forgiving each other…"

Ephesians 5:21 "… be subject to one another …"

Colossians 3:9 "Do not lie to one another…"

Colossians 3:12-13 "bearing with one another and forgiving each other…"

Colossians 3:16 "…teaching and admonishing one another…"

1 Thessalonians 3:12 "…increase and abound in love for one another…"

1 Thessalonians 4:18 "…comfort one another…"

Hebrews 3:13 "…encourage one another…"

Hebrews 10:23-25 "…stimulate one another to love and good deeds…encouraging one other…"

James 4:11 "Do not speak against one another…"

James 5:9 "Do not complain, brethren, against one another..."

James 5:16 "…confess your sins to one another, and pray for one another..."

1 Peter 1:22 "…fervently love one another from the heart,"

1 Peter 4:9 "Be hospitable to one another without complaint."

It could not be more clear. All of these verses work together to eloquently teach us how we are to act and *who* we are to be. God intended these verses for all Christians for all times. We are not excused because we live in the 21st century and are busy. We are to love each other, confess our sins to each other, admonish one another, and build each other up. We are to be involved in one another's lives. It is an obligation and a great blessing for every Christian. I especially like the idea of forbearance. It means that we decide ahead of time to bear with a person before the problem is known. Our decision to love is projected into the future.

Counseling is nothing mysterious. It is not something we need to learn from a university. The "one another" passages are not simply ancient suggestions and helpful tips for living well. They are the formula that psychotherapists have been madly seeking.

In school, I was amazed at the enormous body of work that has been produced in an attempt to discover what helps people overcome problems. The vast ocean of books, professional articles and dissertations has missed the mark in its effort to truly heal broken people. Yet here it is in plain sight for all to see. The fear of the Lord is the beginning of understanding, everything else is just chasing ideas in circles.

These "one-another" passages provide an excellent guide to us as Christians and especially as peer counselors. If you can become adept at fulfilling these passages you will be an excellent counselor and mentor, guaranteed.

Obviously, there are clients who should be referred to professional counselors because of the time demands required for intervention, uncontrolled mental illness, physical dangers to the counselor, etc. Regardless of the severity or nature of the problem, everyone can be helped significantly by following the instruction in these verses.

He Has No Other Plan

Another motivation to offer myself as a counselor is that God has no other plan. I may not always feel like I am going to be able to help someone else, but if God sends me, I will go. He uses His people to do His work. We are the hands, the feet and the listening ears of Jesus to other people. If we do not show up, who will? Perhaps a humanistic counselor who may push immorality in the guise of freedom? A new age counselor who may lead a person away from Jesus and toward a false "messiah?" I have found that many hurting people will not seek professional counseling or help from pastoral staff because they do not think they are important enough to impose on someone's time. Or they simply do not have the resources to pay someone to help them. But they will talk to you. God has divine appointments for each of us.

How Do You Know If You Are Called?

Some people know immediately that they are to be peer counselors when they hear of the idea. Some are intrigued, but need to try it for a while before they know. But here are some qualities I have seen in people who become successful counselors and mentors.

- Do you find that people enjoy talking to you? Before you even realize what is happening, you are listening as someone pours out his life story to you. You may have been doing peer counseling/mentoring for years and not realized it. So if you seem to attract hurting people who want to talk, you are most likely being called to the ministry. Many times others around us see God's gift in us before we do.

- Do you find yourself feeling sad for hurting people and think about them long after you have seen or talked to them? Are you concerned about them after others have forgotten them? This is true for me. When I hear of someone experiencing a difficulty, I can't seem to be able to forget about him for a long time. Others hear about hurting people and let them go from their minds, but I just keep thinking and wondering about them.

- Do you find yourself wanting to do more to help hurting people? You may hear about their struggles and feel that you need to help them. You may have a desire to relate to them on a deeper level but can't find a way into their lives.

Regardless of the signs, you must try. So many people are in misery and suffering alone. They are fighting their battles by themselves and it may be that God has plans for you to help.

There is an urgency to this calling that we cannot overlook. So many times, peer counselors are used in specific times and ways that are supernatural. Don't wait to cram this into the glass jar; make room for it now. Follow your convictions and God will use you.

It is important to note that others may recognize your gift to provide counseling before you see it. I have observed individuals in Soul Care classes who were wondering if they are called to serve as counselors and I was able to see it almost immediately. So **ask others** who know you well. Ask them if you have a gift of listening and validating others who need to talk.

One of the best parts of answering the call is the fulfillment you will receive. I never feel more satisfied and energized than when I am doing what God desires me to do. Paul wrote in Ephesians 2:10 that God has prepared works for us to do ahead of our time. This is amazing. We have a destiny to fulfill in the Kingdom. And when we fulfill this divine destiny, the planets seem to "align." I have heard many testimonies of peer counselors and mentors who say they feel more empowered by offering counseling. It is a stark example of seeing the truth in "it is more blessed to give than to receive." It is not to say that those receiving the counseling are not helped, but those who are offering this service are blessed as well. This is another way to know that you are called. When you are involved in this ministry, you feel energized, empowered, and can't get enough of it.

Go To Where God Is!

Don't we often wonder where God is? We brainstorm for days, create great programs and invite God to bless us in the work. But I think we have it backwards. If we want God's help, should go where He said He would already be.

"The work is extensive and spread out, and we are widely separated from each other along the wall. Wherever you hear the sound of the trumpet, join us there. Our God will fight for us" (Nehemiah 4:19).

The setting for this verse is the story of Nehemiah as he is leading the rebuilding of the walls of Jerusalem. The enemies of the Hebrew people were attacking the city as the Hebrews were trying to rebuild it. When the trumpet sounded, the people were to grab their weapons and rally to where they heard the trumpet sound. God was there and fighting for them.

I love the wisdom that we can glean from this story. God is in the fight! This could not be more true than in this ministry. He is in the fight for failing marriages. He is in the fight for those addicted and those in bondage. He is in the fight for those who are giving up. If we want to be where God is then we go to those people who are in the fight and He will be there. God is with the orphans and the widows in their distress. He is with those in pain and those who are grieving.

A peer counseling ministry is exciting because God is already there and part of it. If you ask and are lonely for God, this may be an answer for you. He is here. He loves you and has a special place in His heart for the people to whom you will be listening. I have witnessed this phenomenon repeatedly. I love it when a new peer counselor calls me after his first appointment and shares how God was present and moving.

One last note about the calling: God does not call the qualified, He qualifies the called. If God asks you to be a peer counselor, He will provide whatever you need. This ministry is difficult, but as time passes and you gain experience the gift within you starts to blossom. This gift is one that needs to be developed and nurtured. At first it may seem awkward, but as you grow it will seem more natural and you will feel more at peace.

Some discover that peer counseling is their unfound purpose. They uncover lost gifts and abilities that God has given to them. When we stretch ourselves to be what God made us to be, He frees us from our self-made prisons of fear and triviality. Once a counselor reaches this state of confidence he is an incredibly powerful force for good in the Kingdom. Let that resonate in your heart and mind; you could be a powerful force in the Kingdom. You could connect with God in a deeper way. You could see Him move and work in someone's life. When we leave our familiar and safe roads to follow God on His narrow one, He promises that we will experience Him. What is better than that? Absolutely nothing!

The following passages speak of God's renewing and refreshing nature. Think and meditate on these for your own spiritual resilience and vitality, and for others to whom you are giving counsel.

Psalms 119:24 "Your statutes are my delight; they are my counselors."

25 "I am laid low in the dust; preserve my life according to your word."

28 "My soul is weary with sorrow; strengthen me according to your word."

32 "I run in the path of your commands, for you have set my heart free."

45 "I will walk about in freedom, for I have sought out your precepts."

50 "My comfort in suffering is this: Your promise preserves my life."

92 "If your law had not been my delight, I would have perished in my affliction."

93 "I will never forget your precepts, for by them you have preserved my life."

108 "Your word is a lamp to my feet and a light to my path."

133 "Direct my footsteps according to your word; let no sin rule over me."

143 "Trouble and distress have come over me, but your commands are my delight."

165 "Great peace have they that love your law, and nothing can make them stumble."

"This is what the Lord says:
Cursed is the one who trusts in man,
who depends on flesh for his strength
and whose heart turns away from the Lord.

He will be like a bush in the wastelands;
he will not see prosperity when it comes.
He will dwell in the parched places of the desert,
in a salt land where no one lives.

But blessed is the man who trusts in the Lord,
whose confidence is in him.

He will be like a tree planted by the water
that sends out its roots by the stream.
It does not fear when heat comes;
its leaves are always green.
It has no worries in a year of drought
and never fails to bear fruit" (Jeremiah 17:5-8).

Chapter 10
Case Studies and Testimonies

These stories from peer counselors and their clients illustrate God working through regular people in extraordinary ways. All identifying information about our clients has been removed or changed to protect their confidentiality.

The following is an e-mail we received as an update regarding a young lady who felt very stuck and separated from God. She was a believer, but needed someone to understand her situation and walk with her through the process of being reunited with her Savior. Her counselor wrote:

I have been working with a woman who was delivered from drugs and alcohol in the past and who has had a very close relationship with Christ. She got involved with a man she worked with and they lived together for two years. This man was an atheist and she walked away from her faith for the time she was with him. She recently ended this relationship but found herself going home from work and drinking each night. She came to us devastated by this behavior and crippled by the fact that she felt she couldn't return to Jesus to ask forgiveness and let Him heal and restore her once again. We asked the Holy Spirit to come into our conversation and direct us. I explained to her that the Word says that, like the prodigal son, she could return and ask for forgiveness. That's what His death on the cross freed us from. We prayed and she asked Jesus to forgive her and heal her. The guilt she was feeling from all this had crippled her so much that she was an easy target for the devil to talk to. I explained that she needed to stop listening to the wrong voice and let God heal and direct her each day. I encouraged her to fill her evenings with family and friends, chores, anything to keep her away from the temptation to drink. Dale had advised her to go to Celebrate Recovery (A faith-based 12 step recovery program) at Canyon View Vineyard Church, which she did.

She has since been attending Celebrate Recovery and has renewed her relationship with her mom, her grown daughter and a couple of good friends. She knew what to do all along but guilt kept her from going forward. She feels she is in good hands with Celebrate Recovery and no longer needs a Soul Care counselor. God is so good.

The Harts are another great example of God using his willing servants. In many ways, the Hart's are a typical church-going couple whose lives are testimonies of righteous living for more than one generation. The spiritual law of sowing and reaping applies here. They, and their families before them, have sown good seed and they are reaping the benefits of reliance on God and hundreds of good decisions. Some would be content with this place in life, but the Harts heard God's call and they responded. They were willing to share themselves with another couple who also understood the spiritual law of sowing and reaping, but from the opposite side. Their lives were riddled with negative consequences of sin and bad choices. The two couples could not have been more different. But through the emotional tension and struggle, God brought them through it all and both couples were blessed. This is their story.

God does not want our marriages to just survive, He wants them to flourish!! With that thought in mind, we got serious about participating in the Marriage Mentoring ministry. Because our marriage has been so special for so long, it broke our hearts that there were so many couples out there whose marriages were languishing or just plain falling apart – how sad that is. Both of us come from stable, loving, nurturing homes which gave us a foundation to build our marriage on, along with lots of Godly role modeling. We had some concerns about relating to these marriages in crisis because we did not have any affairs, drugs, abuse and/or worse in our background . . . how could we even relate to those who experienced any or all of those things? God convinced us that He could use us - not because our marriage was perfect - but because we both had a desire for other couples to experience God in their marriages and we were willing to open up our hearts to love complete strangers. Besides, He was going to give us what we needed to serve Him if this was what He was leading us to participate in; He promises that in His Word.

The most important thing to remember: this is not about us . . . it is about our Heavenly Father wanting to heal some broken hearts and restore love and commitment in marriages that have grown cold. We must be authentic (they know we're not perfect), good listeners (lots of "between the lines" listening), and willing to love these hurting souls with God's love – the very same love He gives to each of us. It is important not to go into this ministry if our own faith is shaky because Satan will have an open door into our hearts to mess with us in any number of ways. We must be ready for God to give our own faith some exercising and we must always be in prayer that our own marriages be protected from the evil one.

We will share our experience with our current couple (J & M) and tell you that we are grateful that they were not our first. Wow! Two very broken people with lots of demons and absolutely no positive role modeling from their very dysfunctional backgrounds. J had already come to Christ in faith, and M shortly after we started meeting with them. But this "faith in God" thing was new to them and because all they had known was the pain of abuse, neglect, drugs, affairs, and many more very bad things they have had to learn and are still learning what a life in Christ is all about and how that relates to their marriage, raising children, etc. They have taken only baby steps forward with lots of giant steps backwards. How do we cope with those times? With lots of prayer and complete reliance in our Creator. We have palpably witnessed God getting a hold of their hearts when a meltdown was about to occur. More than once we witnessed two confused, hurting and selfish people who were ready to walk out on their marriage, but didn't – only God can bring that about in their hearts. We just sat back and marveled at His ministry to their hearts. There were times when we sat in our car after meeting with them and asked each other, "What just happened in there?" That applies to the good times as well as the bad times.

Several things that we have witnessed or experienced:

1. On their first visits, emotional renditions of their stories.

2. There have been times of silence when they have struggled as to what they want to share . . . we have had to give them time to respond or prompt them with another question.

3. We have had to draw out honesty and sometimes participation in this process when one or the other was shut down.

4. We have experienced times of frustration because we sensed a lack of honesty or emotions were getting in the way of real communication with each other.

5. We have had times of amazing improvement followed by more significant problems.

6. Two words, "forgiveness" and "trust," are huge when it comes to this healing process.

7. More than once we witnessed them giving up on themselves, each other and God . . . we silently prayed for God to intervene and give us what we needed so that He could minister to them and, wow, God has always answered those prayers.

There are many more experiences, but during this time we have grown to love two people who are meeting with us for a reason; because God sent them to us. What a privilege to be a part of His amazing plan.

There have been times when we were physically and emotionally spent because of our own days and the thought of meeting with two hurting people wasn't on our list of fun things to do for the evening. But those times seemed to be the best ones when God confirmed to us that we were doing exactly what He wanted us to do and we left with big smiles on our hearts after seeing the Lord work in their lives.

Each story is different and we cannot possibly be prepared for all of the things we will encounter. But, that is okay because it is not about us fixing things, it is about our Heavenly Father working in lives to bring about healing and restoration in their marriages . . . using each of us to minister to the couples that God has entrusted to us. What a privilege that God wants to use us – it truly humbles us.

A happy, healthy marriage that is centered in Christ will have an impact on those who encounter those marriages: children, extended family, neighbors, friends and co-workers. Those encounters are able to make a Kingdom difference; that is what it is all about. The bottom line is bringing glory to our Heavenly Father.

Gordon was one of the original five providers who, by faith, jumped in with both feet and began peer counseling before anyone knew what might happen. We weren't sure if anybody would sign up to see a peer counselor, and if they did sign up we weren't sure exactly what we would do then. God knew the plan and sent many people to us for help. He gave us the time to listen and the words to say. Here is Gordon's account:

I came to the Lord in February of 1991 after going through some rough times and being led to the Lord by my secretary. As I matured in the Lord and continued to go through different trials and tribulations I became more and more aware of God's desire for each of us to help others through their trials and tribulations. He helps us through ours so we can turn around and help others through theirs. I felt for a year or more that I was to help others, but I did not know how.

For several years I was involved in small groups with Dale and knew him and his heart very well. When he put together the first "Peer Counseling Class" I knew I was to take it. The class was primarily to help us learn how to listen to others. I was a small group leader at the time and felt this would help me be a better leader. This was before there was any talk about Soul Care. When the first Soul Care class was established I again signed up and knew I was to be a part of that ministry. I remained an active part of the ministry for about three years and counseled many men.

Some of the men I counseled really didn't know what they wanted out of the counseling session or why they were there. They wanted changes in their lives or wanted to be able to get through their problems, but were not willing to address the causes or put forth the effort needed to work with the Holy Spirit. However, many did want to grow through it and did want to become better men closer to God. It was both a joy and a continued amazement to watch the Holy Spirit conduct the counseling sessions and bring about strength, encouragement, and change in the men who wanted it. Looking back, there were many whose lives were totally changed and made better as a result of the Holy Spirit working through me and the counseling session.

In one case, a marriage that was on the edge of total collapse (the wife was not sure she wanted it restored or even had the strength to work through it), was restored and even made stronger and better. This was accomplished over a period of six to eight months of regular sessions with me and a handoff to another Soul Care provider who specialized in marriage counseling. On several occasions, the individual I was counseling was tired of it all and his wife's unrelenting expectations. He wanted to throw in the towel, but the Holy Spirit had other plans and gave me the words to convey to him that allowed his heart to be receptive to the Holy Spirit's strength to build him up.

In other cases, the marriage or relationship was not restored, but the individual's relationship with Jesus was restored and made even stronger.

There were those I could help and those I could not. I did not take ownership of either. My role was to listen to the Holy Spirit and to the individual I was counseling and be the conduit between the two. My role was to help them see what they could not see, hear what they could not hear, and help them see Jesus working in their lives while getting them to call upon and work with Jesus on their own.

There were times the individual was in such a state that he could not see nor hear anything, so I had to perform spiritual/emotional rescue first aid. Sometimes this meant jumping into the water with him with the Holy Spirit as my life vest and life rope. Sometimes you have to come along side them and walk as they walk and ask the Holy Spirit to let you see what they see and feel what they feel. It is very important though, that this only be done in partnership with the Holy Spirit. To begin with, the individual might hang on to me, but all the time I was holding onto the Holy Spirit and getting him to focus on and turn his attention to Jesus Christ.

I learned through all this that the Holy Spirit does move in peoples lives and that many times when someone is going through something, no matter who they are or how strong their faith is, the situation is so overpowering that they simply cannot see Him. Many times we have to look at it all through their eyes and then be one with them and with the Lord.

I think the biggest and most important principle for a peer counselor to remember is to listen and not judge. We must really listen to what the individual is saying and not saying, and what the Holy Spirit is saying to you and to them. It is so easy to start jumping to conclusions or judgments and totally miss what the Lord really wants to do in their lives and yours.

More times than not, I would have a thought-through plan only to have the Holy Spirit totally change it during the session - sometimes right from the first words spoken. We must remember that the Bible says we are to plan, but the Holy Spirit will direct our steps. We must remain flexible.

As I stated earlier, it was a total joy and amazement to watch the Holy Spirit move and change the individual right before my eyes. In many cases, He changed me and my thinking during the session. I would leave the session and drive home in the clouds. There is nothing better than to be called upon by the living God to be His partner in changing someone's life.

Doug is a youth and family minister at a Church of Christ in Grand Junction, Colorado. The following are Doug's observations regarding the impact of a peer counseling ministry on this church of 300 members.

Soul Care Ministry Summary

I approach this summary with a healthy dose of respect and hesitancy. Writing an opinion of a ministry effort is somewhat like Moses striking the rock in the desert. It borders on assuming I know just what God is up to at every twist and turn in the road and worse, seeks to bring attention to someone other than God Himself. Yet, risking being struck down in mid-keyboard, I trust Jehovah knows I in no way intend to usurp a divine work in progress.

The Soul Care ministry at our church has been active for almost three years and has enabled gifted listeners in our church family to develop their talents while providing an avenue of blessing for others. Many of our providers have been active listeners for years over their kitchen counters, coffee tables and in their living rooms. Soul Care has allowed that informal help to become a more concentrated and deliberate effort. We have asked for God's moment by moment presence in this ministry and have witnessed the Spirit heal and restore lives.

Soul Care has involved some church members in a meaningful and practical ministry effort who may have been only sitting on the pew as mere spiritual spectators. We feel like we are being used and can actually see the results of allowing God to use us. It is encouraging and faith building.

Another area that Soul Care has blessed individuals is in the sharpening of their spiritual sensitivities. It is one thing to admit God works, and quite another thrilling matter altogether to witness God moving firsthand. When providing Soul Care, one cannot help but be tuned into the spiritual battles that rage around us. It shows the truth that, "those who are with us are more than those who are with them" (2nd Chronicles 32:7, 1 John 4:4). Needless to say, such a Kingdom view of each moment, whether in a counseling session or walking through the grocery store, must be close to the path upon which Jesus wants us to trod.

Soul Care has provided a venue for reflective spirituality among our providers. As we help others, our lives have been both blessed and challenged to continue to grow in our faith, slow down, and listen more attentively to our Mighty Counselor and to souls around us. We are more in tune to recognize and praise God for His amazing divine appointments.

How Soul Care has benefited our church as a whole

Soul Care has added a viable, people-oriented ministry to our Kingdom efforts. God is using us to reach out in the name of Christ to the community as well as our own church family. Actually, our providers care for many more among the "un-churched" than among the "churched." In so doing, it is our hope that God will use this Spirit-based counseling to bring them closer to the Kingdom.

This ministry consistently places our church directly and practically in the lives of those to whom Jesus has called us to minister. Soul Care has provided another rallying point for providers to be corporately blessed as they work together, pray together, and discuss together what God may be doing in their clients. A common bond brought about by a common battleground has allowed us to grow closer together in the greater cause of Christ.

Soul Care has allowed our church to interact on a practical level (sharing training, client referrals, etc.) with other churches as we partner in providing. Such a step in uniting at the foot of the cross for a cause greater than our own church traditions certainly comes closer to answering Jesus' prayer for unity among believers.

If I am to be objective in this summary I need to include some challenges we face with our Soul Care ministry: we have not been able to retain all those providers who initially showed interest and went through the Soul Care 101 training.

Fending off provider discouragement through seasons of lesser activity has been somewhat challenging. In order to counter these effects we meet regularly regardless of lulls in counseling activity. As we meet, we remind ourselves we are Spirit warriors ready to enter the fight at a moment's notice and therefore down time is God time.

So, even through seasons of decreased activity we meet, we pray, we seek God's guidance and ask to be used at His discretion and according to His time.

For some reason, it seems we must constantly remind our own church members of the availability of the Soul Care ministry that is right before them. Of course, not as many as we would like take advantage of the ministry. And, of course, we trust God to send us clients as His will dictates.

As a minister, I seek to engage disciples in meaningful, practical service that will develop a deeper long term trust in the intricate and often subtle workings of Jehovah. God is using our Soul Care ministry to mature us, make us more patient, more attentive and more sensitive to His Kingdom on earth. Everyone is blessed because we are also able to care for souls in a way that will make an eternal difference to him.

Doug touched on many great blessings of a peer counseling ministry. I especially want to highlight how God has worked *among* the churches in our community. I do not think God sees the outside walls of our buildings as we do. He sees His believers as a whole and desires for us to work as one. We see this happening in our peer counseling ministries because we refer back and forth as there is availability and suitability of providers. For example, we may have a Spanish speaking client and need to refer to a provider in another church who has that ability. Or we may we have an older couple that needs help and know that an older couple is available at another church. Occasionally, a client may prefer to speak to someone who does not see him and his friends at church every week. We make referrals based on availability, and we trust God is arranging His Divine appointments.

Pat is truly a Godly woman who brightens any room she walks into. She was the first volunteer to accept an assignment, and God showed Himself that day. Because of her boldness and her servant heart, many have followed and have been blessed by our loving God.

My journey with Soul Care takes me back many years now! The Holy Spirit encouraged me to take a leap of faith and that's just what I did. After completing several Soul Care classes, I knew beyond a shadow of a doubt that Soul Care was to be my ministry and calling.

The Lord has been gracious in presenting to me so many wonderful and challenging women to talk to! It has been one of the most enriching and rewarding experiences of my life. I cannot remember a time when I've been happier and I now know it's in serving that we see our Lord's beauty and grace! My prayer is to have enough time to truly fulfill my calling and help as many people as God will allow. If this ministry has taught me anything, it is understanding what humility is and seeing God's immense love for us!

Helen was one of the first providers in the ministry. She is a warm and inviting person who I can always trust to support other women through very difficult times. She can connect well even with women who are remarkably different from her in life circumstances and personality. Her gifts and her willingness to use them make her a mighty soldier on our team. I asked her to give a sample of the clients that she has seen.

I am a 63 year old mother of 4 grown children with 6 wonderful grandchildren. I accepted Christ as my savior 33 years ago and I enjoy a precious relationship with Him. I see my primary ministry as helping and supporting my family. In addition to the ministry to my family, I became involved in supporting people in crisis. God made it clear to me that this was my gifting and when our family moved to the Grand Junction area I was one of the first few to begin peer counseling at the Canyon View Vineyard Church.

I have met with many ladies over the years and have learned to listen, listen, listen with my heart and soul and spirit. One lady came to our ministry asking for help and support as she went through a divorce from a husband who was an alcoholic. She had four children, no money and was scared and overwhelmed. I simply set out to be a person to whom she could talk and feel no judgment. She had many bumps in the road, but as we went together through the trials, we saw our prayers answered, her faith and self confidence grow, and we became very close. We prayed together, and I prayed on my own as well. Over the one year period that we met together, God brought her and her children through a real difficult time. I was truly blessed, myself, to be a part of her story.

Not all counseling relationships are as ideal. I met with a woman who had been to many other counselors in the community before seeking help from our ministry. Her husband had an affair and she was extremely angry. During our meetings it was difficult to keep her from constantly bad-mouthing her husband. We worked on her appropriately expressing her anger, and also worked on forgiveness and scripture that was relevant. She began growing in her self esteem as it related to her identity in Christ. She would take some steps forward and then go back to attacking her husband, almost as if she had forgotten all that we had worked on. She seemed more interested in staying where she was in the toxic thoughts rather than moving toward a place where she could move forward and closer to God.

In cases like these, I have to remind myself to see people as God sees them. I did not feel judgment or condemnation toward her, but began to feel as though I was working harder than she was. After meeting together for eight months, we amicably decided to end our sessions together. I am only God's vehicle and cannot fall into the trap of thinking I can "fix" all the problems. I can keep leading my clients back toward God and his Word, but cannot feel responsible if they do not want to stay there. God knows everyone's heart and whether they are ready for change. My part is to be faithful to listen and to encourage, and to not be so invested in how it is received.

I met with another lady who was very tearful about her daughter who was using drugs and was pregnant out of wedlock. During our meetings she cried and cried. She was full of anger, fear, and frustration. She needed to vent all her feelings and I encouraged her to do so. Over the weeks that we met together, she began to see the blessings in her life and she began to rely more on God. We focused on scripture that brought her peace and comfort. Her life circumstances did not change, but her relationship with God did. After meeting together for 7 or 8 months she felt stronger in her faith to the degree we decided to discontinue our meetings. I saw her a year later at church. When she noticed me, she had a big smile on her face and introduced me to her baby granddaughter. I was truly blessed to see her continuing to praise God.

Jeffrey is a single man with many talents. It is a blessing to have spirit-led men like Jeffrey who can step into another man's life, spend the time necessary to listen, and give Godly counsel in a world full of highly distracted and lost men.

I have served in several different capacities in the church including grief support groups, volunteer carpentry, singles ministry, ushering, choir vocals, and have helped facilitate holiday memorial services. But none presented more of a challenge to my abilities than Soul Care. When I first became involved, I felt intimidated. However, after going through some training I gained soulful understanding that it was not about me providing my own answers, but exploring answers with another person and looking to God for direction and counsel. It helps to know that I don't have to give the answers. I just have to be willing to stand arm and arm with someone as we both learn by exploring and seeking God's direction. I have always been a person who likes to discuss meaningful things in life. It is a freeing and rewarding experience to allow God to use me to encourage others.

In today's society, we are often rushed from one thing to another and seldom devote the appropriate time to really listen to other people. With a clear understanding of how to actually "hear" someone, it is amazing how willing people are to sort through their own issues with help and directional guidance from God. It is helpful and healing for not only the client, but also for the peer counselor.

Donna and Gary are excellent examples of people with ordinary backgrounds whom God has brought into the ministry. Gary works at a utility company and Donna works in the payroll office at a local college. They are empty-nesters who desire to work together in service for God. This is a summary of their first assignment; a troubled couple they worked with approximately ten times.

When our church asked for couples interested in serving as peer counselors, I felt a tug at my heart to volunteer with the ministry. However, Gary was not sure counseling was something he could do or would be effective at. After praying about it, we both decided to sign up for the training.

Once we completed peer counseling training, Gary actually felt as though God could use him to mentor others. Dale's training was easy to understand and he presented it in a way that we felt comfortable that it was something we could do.

One of the things that stood out for me was God's divine plan. As I look back on our peer counseling experience, I see that God used us to help a couple who was struggling through some of the same issues we had gone through in our relationship. God not only used our peer counseling to mentor another couple in their marriage, but also in their spiritual lives. It was a natural progression to discuss their relationship with God as we shared some of our own experiences with them; in fact, many times they brought it up themselves.

Gary and I would both agree that we were blessed more than the couple we mentored. God used our time with them to strengthen our own relationship with each other and also with God. Quite honestly, sometimes you really don't know what to say or do and it was during those sessions that we prayed hard! God was there, and each time He gave one of us words to say that brought peace, reconciliation or even accepted confrontation. It was not our great skill by any means, but it was God's power and grace, and we were privileged to be a part of it.

In one of our sessions, our couple started off by thanking us for our time and help. They stated that they had been in four previous counseling experiences and had never really received much help. This was their last attempt to make things work and they said that for the first time they really felt they had learned a lot that could affect their marriage in a positive way. What hit me hard at that moment was, "Wow! I could have missed this!" God could have done this without us, but because we stepped out nervously in faith, God allowed us to be used by Him to affect a positive change in the lives of real people. Gary and I got to be a part of that!

The church is called to share God's love, and for us, peer counseling is a natural extension of just that: loving people enough to give of your time to help and support them through crises and to be blessed in the process.

Bob Clifford is the Outreach Pastor at the Canyon View Vineyard Church in Grand Junction, Colorado and has been one of the ministry's strongest supporters. Here are some words from Bob.

Soul Care fulfills Ephesians 4:11-13: "So Christ Himself gave the apostles, the prophets, the evangelists, the pastors and teachers, to equip His people for works of service, so that the body of Christ may be built up until we all reach unity in the faith and in the knowledge of the Son of God and become mature, attaining to the whole measure of the fullness of Christ."

The opinion of the unchurched is that the church is irrelevant to help them with any part of their personal lives. This belief is substantiated due to the saints not being "trained for service." Soul Care runs contrary to this trend by offering a service at no cost that helps people with their real needs: to be better parents, have better marriages, and seek real and abiding relationships with their eternal Father.

Most of the "pastors" in the church are not paid professionals. They are members of the church who are given gifts by God to serve in His church. Peer counselors in the Soul Care ministry are serving in pastoral roles. Realistically, a paid pastor from the Vineyard can only spend an hour or two with someone and meet with him only a few times. Every church group is forced to make a decision about how to meet the counseling needs of its members. They will either hire a professional counselor, or do nothing. Peer counseling ministries give a third option for a church. Peer counselors can meet with them as much as needed over long periods of time. It is practically impossible for any church leader to commit this amount of time to the number of folks who truly need the help. Sheer numbers alone make the case that peer counseling is the best answer for meeting the needs of the people. All the clergy and Christian professional counselors together are simply not enough.

Soul Care meets the needs of those seeking help and provides an avenue for other members to use their gifts to pastor and shepherd. It is a "win-win" situation and God is glorified. Tell me what is more needed in this world than that?

Chapter 11
Why Organize into a Ministry?

I not only use all the brains that I have, but all that I can borrow.

Woodrow Wilson

Nehemiah was a great leader. His heart was broken over a problem and he prayerfully approached the solution. He planned, organized, persevered and overcame. This story in scripture is a great blueprint for any ministry. It shows how God works through organization and plans, and how we need to ask God to be present. Some Christians have good intentions but resist organization and planning. They believe God will be constrained by it. Others organize and plan to the extent there is no room for God to work at all. Like Nehemiah, we must organize, plan **and** be sensitive to God's leading.

My goal for this chapter is to explain how to build an effective ministry that will last. Peer counseling is difficult. Without a plan and some organization, the peer counselors will not stay committed. They will burn out, feel discouraged, and drop out of service. But with the proper structure and support they will have an opportunity to serve in the ministry for many years with confidence and enthusiasm. It is all about sustainability.

I realize that not every reader will be a part of a body that can build a complete ministry. Some churches are just too small or do not have the support or resources for this undertaking. Regardless of the church body in which God has placed you, His Great Spirit will help you. He is very interested in this ministry because it reaches his favored people: the downcast and troubled. God's heart for those in pain is seen everywhere in scripture. God hears the prayers of His people and hears every word uttered by those suffering. He will be ready to indwell you and this ministry to help these hurting people.

Therefore, we need to meet Him as prepared as we can be, so His power can be seen and His name glorified. I'm not a Christian who believes we are to go forward in ministry recklessly and without a plan. We organize and plan, but all is done in faith, in prayer, in wisdom and careful attention to scripture. God's Spirit will pilot this ship and make course corrections as needed. Our job is to pay attention to Him and His leadership. This flexibility is sometimes difficult to embrace, but it is essential for success. The following information explains how The Canyon View Vineyard Church in Grand Junction organized this ministry, but your system may look different. God may have a different plan for you. You have a different facility and have different people with different gifts. But the result should be the same; everyone involved is drawn closer to God and troubled people are greatly blessed. In this chapter I will refer to the ministry as "Soul Care," but you may call your ministry anything you choose.

I. THE NUTS AND BOLTS

Liability

Most churches already have insurance policies in place to cover general liability issues and may have liability coverage for the paid staff. Check with your church's carrier about a peer counseling ministry and how it may be covered. It is my understanding that peer counseling is seen no differently than church small groups or prayer meetings. We are "nonprofessionals" ministering in church settings and do not charge for services. You may be advised, as we were, to administer the ministry within your own facility. This helps to differentiate us from professional counselors who carry professional liability coverage and who typically operate in business settings. We live in a litigious society and, therefore, need to be wise and protect ourselves. "I am sending you out like sheep among wolves. Therefore, be as shrewd as snakes and as innocent as doves" (Matthew 10:16).

Another protection from litigation is to be crystal-clear about who we are and what we are trained to do and not do. Our best tool to accomplish this is our Information Sheet. (Figure 11.1) This is read aloud in the first appointment with each new client. The peer counselor answers any questions the clients may have, and then the Information Sheet is signed. We keep the signed copy and we make sure each client has a copy to take home so he will have the emergency numbers to reference if needed.

Counseling Boundaries

We have found that the Information Sheet accomplishes several very important things. First, it puts everyone more at ease during the first appointment when there tends to be some anxiety. The clients learn there is no fee for the service, and also learn the limits of confidentially. We also use this form to set boundaries. For example, the form clearly states that we do not accept crisis calls and they are advised to call 911 or the community crisis number if they are experiencing an emergency. Emergency work is more taxing on our time and our emotions and is best left to crisis professionals. The last sentence in this form speaks to our expectation of the clients to respect the volunteers' time. It is not uncommon for people to set appointments and then not show up or call to cancel. This is an ongoing issue for us, and this form is one way we have found to minimize it.

Figure 11.1

Soul Care Ministries

General Information

Welcome to Soul Care at the Canyon View Vineyard Church. We would like to share the following information about our ministry.

1. The information you share with your Soul Care Provider is <u>Confidential</u>. Only under extreme situations such as child abuse or strong suicidal/homicidal thoughts will we share information with others. Some information may also be shared with a Soul Care supervisor.

2. There is no fee for this service. We are Christians who love the Lord Jesus and want to serve Him by listening and offering encouragement. We are not professional counselors and are not trained to perform emergency services. For emergencies, please **call 911** or the community **Emergency Services and Suicide Prevention number, 000-0000.**

3. Please call us if you are not able to make your scheduled appointment. Call any number your peer counselor has given you to cancel or reschedule. Thank you for respecting our limited space and time.

Signature

This document is not legal advice and should not be taken as such. This is simply what we do to inform people of who we are and what to expect.

Course work

There are three phases of training for the Soul Care Providers to complete. We call them Soul Care 101, Soul Care 201 and Soul Care 301.

Soul Care 101 is directed toward people who are interested in joining the ministry or wish to learn more about it. Most individuals come with curiosity and doubts about their abilities. The 101 course provides foundational scriptures that speak of our mission and equip us for the work of counseling. We also practice active listening exercises. Much of the material that is taught in Soul Care 101 is included in this book. We have taught this class in a weekly format for 6 to 8 consecutive weeks for an hour each night, and have also offered it in a combined 3 hour Friday night and 3 hour Saturday morning format. The latter seems to be better attended.

Soul Care 201 is the practicum. This class meets once per week and gives the students frequent contact with more experienced counselors and supervisors. Some students prefer to wait until they feel more at ease to take an assignment, but after listening to the experiences of others they usually jump in. Assignments are given, and the "cases" are discussed in group supervision settings each week. The people about whom we share information remain anonymous due to our commitment to confidentiality. We do not use names, but rather focus on the peer counselor's role and level of comfort in the process rather than details about the case. At this point, specific questions arise from the peer counselors regarding various aspects of counseling. We take these opportunities to provide further education. The students share the responsibility of researching and finding answers. They learn the value of continuing education, seeking information on their own, and sharing with others. We are stronger together and need each other to be effective peer counselors. Some scripture to consider:

"Two are better than one, because they have a good return for their work: If one falls down, his friend can help him up. But pity the man who falls and has no one to help him up! Also, if two lie down together, they will keep warm. But how can one keep warm alone? Though one may be overpowered, two can defend themselves. A cord of three strands is not quickly broken" (Ecclesiastes 4:9-12).

"Plans fail for lack of counsel, but with many advisers they succeed" (Proverbs 15:22).

These are the reasons we meet as a group and work on solutions and plans for our clients together. The 201 class meets weekly until the participants feel they are ready to advance to the 301 class. Some classes choose to move on after approximately 6 weeks while other groups have met for two months or longer. We stay flexible and try to accommodate the needs of the new providers.

Soul Care 301 is the working ministry. These peer counselors and mentors meet once per month. The format is very similar to 201 meetings. They discuss cases and get ideas and encouragement from one another. These meetings are a great source of encouragement and support. I always feel uplifted when I hear the stories the providers tell of God moving and working among those seeking help. We work hard on every case and develop a plan for each counselor to implement for the people they are working to help. God uses our combined wisdom and experiences to help people.

The 201 and the 301 groups are both overseen by professional counselors. This is done in our group by professionals who volunteer their time and expertise. It is important to have them present, or at least available, for consultation if the need arises, but I do not believe they should give the majority of the feedback. They are present to ensure the cases are appropriate for peer counselors and to answer ethical or legal questions. As you have read in previous chapters, God is the mighty counselor and will guide us. Professional counselors have a role to play in the ministry, but they are not almighty.

The Warm Line

The contact point for those seeking our counsel is a cell phone designated for our ministry. We hand out business cards with this number to people we meet in our daily activities who may need some soul care. (Figure 11.2) These cards can also be placed in prayer rooms and distributed to church members to hand out. At different times, we also have brochures and announcements in bulletins to get our phone number out to our church members.

We call this the "warm line" because we do not answer immediately, but return calls within 24 hours. The greeting on the phone instructs the caller to leave a message so we can return the call. Most emergency calls are eliminated because of the delay in response. An example of a greeting on the phone would be, "Thank you for calling the Soul Care Ministry, please leave your name and number and we will call you back soon. If this is an emergency, please call 911."

Fig 11.2

SOUL CARE MINISTRY

*Peer Counseling for Couples
and Individuals*

Canyon View Vineyard Church
736 24 1/2 Road
Grand Junction, Co 81505

(000) 000-0000   *Free Service*

Key People

Every person in this ministry is important. When someone is missing from his or her post, it is felt by everyone. This ministry is quintessential of the body metaphor used by Jesus to describe the church. We have identified five necessary "positions" in this ministry. You may find that one person is able to assume more than one of these positions, or each of these positions may be assumed by a different person. We like to spread out the responsibilities as much as possible. In choosing people for each of these positions, keep in mind the gifts of each of person and match him to the work.

Soul Care Providers are those who have completed the course work and practicum and provide counseling and mentoring. Some are interested in doing individual counseling, while others work with their spouses to provide marriage mentoring. Some have the flexibility to do both. These Soul Care Providers are the heart of the ministry and have personal contact with those seeking help.

This is a good place to discuss the differences between counseling and mentoring; both of these words have broad definitions and have different meanings to different people. The greatest difference to me is that mentoring involves more sharing by the one offering help. Married couples tend to offer more mentoring due to the fact they are both present and can model the marital relationship since that is the issue. While mentoring does occur when working with individuals, frequently the relationship is primarily focused on the one seeking help. The individual who is offering counsel may not have specific experience with the issue brought by the one seeking help. At times, we also refer to these relationships as discipleship and life coaching. Regardless of what you choose to call these relationships, they are the core of the ministry.

Figure 11.4 is a handout we give to the providers explaining the steps to get started. (Your form will, of course, look different, but it is a guideline from which to work.) The rest of the positions that follow serve as support and keep the providers working in the most effective way possible.

The Trainer is the person who teaches the materials and scriptures to the Soul Care Providers. This person must, obviously, have the gift of teaching and have the ability to encourage and inspire those who are interested in learning. This person must also have experienced success as a counselor and mentor. Many of the students have doubts and insecurities about sitting down with someone they have not met to offer help in his life and walk with the Lord. The trainer also works as a shepherd to those in the ministry. He or she develops relationships with the students as they attend the classes and learn their interests and gifts. Some students may have personal issues that create obstacles to working as volunteers in the ministry. The trainer may need to offer help to them to overcome their own issues in order to be part of the ministry.

It is important that this person has the ability to not only provide the information, but also be able to nurture the students to fulfill their purposes in the ministry. Some individuals who attend the training may not have the gift to work in the ministry.

We have found that most people who are not gifted to perform peer counseling are not interested in the classes and soon drop out on their own. For the few who may still want to serve but are not suited for the work, the trainer will respectfully redirect them to a ministry where they are better gifted to serve.

The Screener serves as the front door to the ministry. It is his or her responsibility to return calls from the "warm line." He or she determines the callers' issues and decides which provider is best suited to give them the help they need. If they are not appropriate for the ministry, they are referred to other ministries or to other resources in the community. Because of this screening and referral process, it is important for the screener to be informed of the resources available in the community, including services offered by other churches and professionals. The following list includes issues that we have chosen not to address because we know others can better help in these areas.

- Crisis counseling
- Recent suicide attempts or strong suicidal thoughts
- Recent domestic violence
- Long term drug addiction
- Significant untreated medical problems
- Significant mental illness
- Homicidal thoughts and feelings

We have helped people deal with these issues to some degree, but when they are the predominate problems we refer to professional counselors or appropriate support groups in the community. For example, if drug addiction is the primary issue then we refer them to the local chapter of Celebrate Recovery. This Christ-based recovery program is better suited to help those with pervasive addictions and the issues related to recovery. We limit the work of Soul Care to the areas where we can be the most effective.

The Soul Care screening form (Figure 11.3) provides structure for our phone conversations and helps determine a caller's appropriateness for our ministry. We have found that most callers fit our acceptance criteria and are brought into our peer counseling ministry. Once someone is accepted, the screener calls a Soul Care provider, gives him information from the screening form (Figure 11.3) and has the provider call to set up an appointment. The screener also follows up with the provider to ensure that contact has been made so that anyone needing help can have someone to talk with quickly.

The gifts needed by a screener are varied. The person needs to be organized and detail oriented and also able to show compassion and empathy. He/she also needs to be persistent in calling everyone involved and knowledgeable about the providers so a good match between the caller and the provider can be made. This is something that we pray about. We want God to direct our decisions when matching callers and providers. This position was initially filled by volunteers who had time available as it was required. As the number of calls increased, a paid staff member took the responsibilities as part of his or her position at the church.

The volunteer coordinator has the responsibility of keeping track of those working in the ministry. This is not an easy assignment and can be compared to herding cats. This person communicates to the volunteers when classes are offered and when the supervision groups meet. Along with the screener, he tracks who has assignments and whether they are attending the appropriate meetings. We want to ensure that our peer counselors are in regular contact with others in the ministry, especially when they have assignments. We also are mindful that volunteers have competing time demands and occasionally need breaks from providing services. At these times they are put on "inactive status" with an estimated time for returning to service.

Another important responsibility of the coordinator is to recruit new volunteers for the ministry. This is usually done through the church's publications and through the in-house media. A list is kept of those interested in the training so they may be contacted when training is offered.

All of these positions are important for the ministry to function effectively. As previously mentioned, one person may be able to fulfill the duties of more than one position, but it is best to spread out the responsibilities to others if practical.

Figure 11.3

SOUL CARE SCREENING PROFILE

Date_____

Name _____

Age_____

Address_____

Phone (Home) _____ (Work) _____ (Cell) _____

May we leave messages at these numbers? _____

Vocation _____

Marital Status _____

Has there been any domestic violence? _____

Have you been married previously? _____

If you are seeking marriage counseling are both spouses willing

to attend? _____

Spouse/Partner

 Name_____

Age_____

Spouse's Vocation_____

Children_____

What would you like to talk about in counseling?

_____

_____

_____

Counseling History

_____

_____

Medical Concerns

_____

_____

Medications

_____

Drug and Alcohol use

_____

Are you experiencing any suicidal thoughts?

_____ None _____ Passing _____ Persistent

Church Attendance

_____

Appointment preferences (days and times)

_____

How did you hear about our ministry?

_____

Figure 11.4

Procedures for Soul Care Providers

1. All potential Soul Care providers are expected to attend the 101 and 201 training classes. We understand that everyone is busy, so the information and the process to become a counselor/mentor are very condensed. Therefore, it is essential to attend each class.

2. After completing the necessary coursework you may receive an assignment. Using the numbers provided, call the person and introduce yourself as a Soul Care Provider. Schedule a time when you both can meet. When leaving messages, be general about who you are: others in the household may not be aware someone is seeking counseling. For example, you might say, "Hello this is Dale from the Canyon View Vineyard Church and I am calling John about the Soul Care ministry. Please call me back at (Phone #.)" If you cannot get a response after three attempts and have double-checked the phone numbers with the screener for accuracy, advise the screener of these attempts and tell him of your availability for another assignment.

3. If you do make contact and set a meeting time, call the appropriate staff member to request a meeting room.

4. It is our policy to hold Soul Care and Marriage Mentoring meetings at the church building. We have been encouraged to meet "on campus" for insurance and liability reasons. We do not always know those who are seeking help and do not know what kind of boundaries they are capable of keeping. Safety is a priority.

We discourage meeting in homes because they can be full of distractions: children, parcel deliveries, the phone, etc. In some cases, the home environment actually prevents people from going to deeper levels of disclosure. Homes are comfortable and convenient, but the problems that could arise with home meetings often offset the convenience.

5. At the first meeting with the client, <u>read to them</u> the Soul Care General Information Form.

A.) Ask the client to sign a copy for Soul Care records.

B.) Give the client a copy so he/she will have the emergency numbers available.

6. Should an emergency arise with someone you have been assigned (suicidal/homicidal thoughts, child abuse, etc.) please call one of the numbers listed below. If you are not sure whether your situation is an emergency, call anyway to get another opinion on the matter. (Provide several numbers of people or local agencies that could be contacted for reporting emergencies and for consultation.)

Marketing Examples

The following are examples of a submission for a church bulletin.

Did You Know?

We need each other. Many of us fight our greatest battles all alone . . . but we don't have to.

Soul Care Ministry is here to help. We are peer counselors who are ready to truly listen to you. It is confidential, and there is no charge.

Call 000-0000 to schedule an appointment.

You'll be glad you did.

Relationship problems?

Call 000-0000 to make an appointment with a peer counselor. There is no fee for this service.

Chapter 12
Marriage Mentoring

In my experience, most people who call a Christian peer counseling ministry are either couples or individuals who are seeking help in their marital relationships. I chose to include a separate chapter on marriage mentoring because it has unique qualities from other forms of peer counseling. Marriage mentors are couples who work with another couple or family. Those who counsel couples rather than individuals may face unique challenges: the dynamics between couples can be more complex and the counseling process typically has a greater element of self disclosure. The program also requires a greater degree of flexibility when offering help for the variety of the problems that couples present.

With married couples seeking counseling, there is a wide range in the severity of the problems. Some couples have minor difficulties that can be discussed in a few appointments then they are back on course, managing quite well on their own. Other couples may not be able to rationally converse and cannot even be in the same room together.

If you are starting a new peer counseling ministry, you will need to begin with one level of care and expand as you have workers and interest. Work with your volunteers as the Lord enables you and feel satisfied with what you are able to do. On the following pages I describe the levels of care so you have an idea of what is possible, but don't let this list limit your work. Many other possibilities exist.

Premarital Counseling is accomplished through classes or through married couples meeting with those who are considering marriage. Various materials are available, but it is recommended that you find a God-centered approach. Not all Christian material is strong in its spiritual and scriptural approach. We have used *Prepare to Last* [1] which is a nine week program that involves watching DVD's in class and completing assigned homework. As the need arises, the couples who attend the classes have the option to meet with the class instructors to help sort through their particular issues in private settings. This class has been fruitful in helping couples realize what is necessary to make a relationship work, and in some instances they have decided not to continue their relationships.

Marriage Keepers offers marriage mentoring to newly married couples. Once a couple is married they are assigned a mentoring couple. The mentoring couple calls to introduce themselves to the newlyweds then offers to stop by and visit with a gift, usually a picture frame or other appropriate gift. The newly married couple is expecting this call because they are informed of the ministry in their premarital class or by a church pastor who is performing premarital counseling. They become acquainted and the mentoring couple gives them a business card-sized refrigerator magnet with their names and picture on it (Figure 12.1). This magnet keeps the mentoring couple ever present in their minds.

This relationship is designed to provide mentors who the newly married couples can call for safe and unbiased support. The purpose is to encourage the new couple during the first year of marriage, but it may develop into a relationship that lasts for several years or even a lifetime. Some of the couples meet on a regular basis while others decide to meet on an "as needed" basis. If a couple experiences substantial difficulties, then a referral is made to a higher level of care within the peer counseling ministry.

Figure 12.1

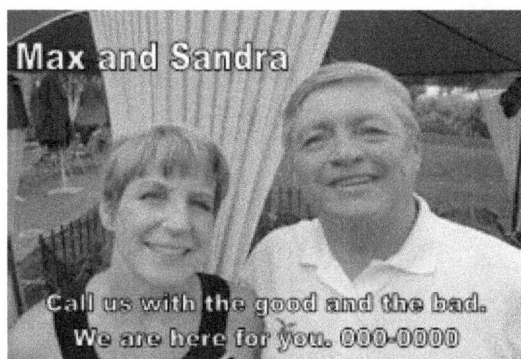

Max and Sandra

Call us with the good and the bad.
We are here for you. 000-0000

Marriage Mentors are couples who work with a husband and wife who need help with their relationship but are calm enough to discuss issues together. We have found that most couples seeking help fall into this category. They may argue frequently, have issues with extended family members, have blended family issues, experience general marital unhappiness, and many times have several issues that need attention all at once. But they are able to work together on their problems with some degree of success. If a couple simply cannot get along well enough to sit in the same room, we refer them to one-on-one counseling with a peer counselor or perhaps a professional counselor.

Mentoring couples go through basic peer counseling training to gain the foundational skills for this work, but ultimately each couple develops their own style of peer counseling based on their personal experience.

Some couples are in a state of crisis or separation. They cannot productively be in the same room and carry on a conversation, but it is still possible to help them. It is not uncommon for us to receive a call from someone who has recently discovered that his or her spouse is having an affair so they are separated and not speaking to each other. In these situations we have tried various methods, but have found the *Marriage 911 First Response*[2] materials to be the most useful. We do not use all of the materials, but have found the workbooks to be especially helpful in working with the spouses individually when that is the only option. Even if only one member of the couple wants to participate, he or she can go through the material and the marriage can be blessed by it. There is a danger, however, that when couples receive counseling apart from each other the chance of divorce may increase or conflict may be prolonged. This may occur when counselors are not diligent to keep the focus on the individual's responsibilities in the relationship. The session can easily lead to bashing the other spouse. Stick to the weekly topics and assignments. This will keep the focus on God and on the individual's responsibilities, and will prevent the topics from becoming destructive to the marriage. We have used these materials while working with each member of a couple individually and also used them until both individuals are willing to work together with a mentoring couple.

Professional counselors are available for consultation and referrals. As noted earlier, in many situations peer counselors may be equally or more effective than paid counselors. God will work through all types of people or couples so do not be too quick to send away someone who needs help.

Marriage mentoring is effective, especially through perseverance and prayer. However, for reasons previously mentioned, some couples are not appropriately served by a volunteer ministry. Callers who are screened out of the peer counseling ministry should be referred to professional counselors. Be sure the professional counselors to whom you send people value your peer counseling ministry and hold true Christian beliefs. Because of their education and training, it is not uncommon for counselors to hold humanistic and new age beliefs so it is important to interview and screen the professionals you are sending clients to for help.

The *Marriage Mentoring Appointment Outline* (Figure 12.2) is a helpful tool for marriage mentors to begin their work. It provides structure for the first appointment. This form encourages you to share some about your own life. It will lower the tension in the room by letting them know with whom they are about to share personal information. Always ask them, along the way, if they have any questions. At this point it is helpful to get some general information about each of their backgrounds and record it in the form of a genogram (see Chapter 8). This is a concise way to keep track of names, children, step children, previous marriages, etc. which can be very confusing. I use only a few of the symbols from this system, but it does help me stay mentally organized during a session, and helps refresh my memory from prior appointments. A genogram also gives you a chance to look at their families of origin, which is where they have learned about relationships.

If you have not done so already, ask them what they want to talk about. List the problems they are experiencing on one side of the page and, more importantly, write their strengths on the other. This will help you from the onset of counseling to believe there is hope for the couple to overcome their difficulties. To get further information, ask them the questions listed on the sheet. Have each of them answer each question, especially if one member of the couple is quieter than the other. This should help you get started and assist in obtaining useful information about your couple.

Figure 12.2

Marriage Mentoring Appointment Outline

Names:_____

Date:_____

1. Read and Discuss the <u>General Information Sheet</u> so the client will understand the nature of the counseling relationship and its boundaries.

    A. Keep signed copy.

    B. Give client a copy.

2. Share personal information about yourself and your marriage.

3. Ask if they have any questions about you or the ministry.

4. Draw a family outline that includes their families of origin.

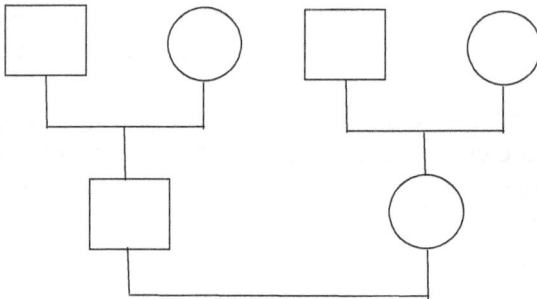

5. Ask what they want to talk about and record information below. Listen for the two stories.

Problems	God's Spirit at Work

6. Questions

(Be sure to record answers for each question from each member of the couple.)

- What needs to be different in your relationship?
- What does God need to do in your relationship?
- What can the husband do to love his wife more?
- What can the wife do to respect her husband more?
- How is your relationship with God?
- How can we pray for you this week?

Marriage mentoring is effective, very Biblical, and is something in which I believe God has great interest. You may find it both difficult and rewarding all in the same moment. Beginning and building a marriage mentoring program is a great undertaking, but there are very few things in life that can bring more blessings to others as well as to ourselves.

Chapter 13
Final Encouragement

The church consists of the people; not the buildings, programs and Sunday services. We are the church that God uses to bless the world by bringing His word and showing them Jesus, our savior. God has no other plan. Scary isn't it? Some days I want to challenge the wisdom of this plan, but I know God has it all worked out. I trust Him with this big mess we made.

One key aspect of His plan is for us to help others. He wants us to pick up these people who are struggling with sin, who are confused about God, and who have given up hope that God loves them at all. The work of caring for troubled souls is critical and so important, but I fear we have given it to others who do not really have what is needed to help hurting people.

It is time to reclaim territory that we have given up. Simply put, the church needs to repent. We need to turn around and face the facts. The church is viewed as a relic from the past that has grown irrelevant. At some level, Christians may believe this as well. When someone is crying or upset do we talk with them? Or do we think, "Send them downtown for some professional help?" If we want others to believe that the Gospel is relevant to this world, we have to first believe it ourselves.

Once we believe with our head and hearts that God's message is exactly what people need for their "psychological" problems, then we must vigorously fight for our right to care for the soul. It was our God-given domain first, and we must take it back.

What does this mean for you? Does it mean you will go to the person with a tear in his eye and ask what is wrong? Will you make that phone call to the family that just lost someone, or to the family that everyone knows is having problems, but is afraid to call? Maybe you will bring people together to form a support group for teen mothers, or for people going through divorces, or suffering from illness. Maybe you will gather others in a class and start listening to each other and "practice" to prepare yourselves to listen to strangers. Maybe you are the one who gathers people together and meets with a church leader to say, "We must act, how do we start?"

History has shown that great and notable men and women have made differences in many ways for the betterment of the world. But a closer examination of history reveals that it is the common citizens of the world who cumulatively make the most extreme impact. God is using people like you and me to shape history and to keep the gospel seed planted, watered and harvested. In the quiet back rooms of church buildings and in the living rooms of the chosen, the words of scripture are being lived out. These listening ears are tools in the Carpenter's hands, healing and sculpting hearts.

The way to conquer in this battle for the soul is to be humble. It is a true paradox, for sure. To win the great battle, we must drop our guns, pick up the towel of the servant and wash feet. We must do the dirty work that only the lowest of servants will do. This work is to listen. Just listen. Hear the hurt, the pain, and the feelings of hopelessness and deep frustration. And that is when the mighty power of God is released. By this simple selfless act of listening, the hard, cruel world is cracked open for the gospel to enter.

One soul at a time, the world sees Jesus. The war for the soul of man will not be fought by great powers and gunships, it will be fought by humble followers of Jesus. This is how God will take back the ground we have surrendered to the enemy. We must model the open heart of Jesus as we go through life with the modern day woman at the well, the beggar at the gate, and the thief on the cross. These people walk among us, not knowing the wonderful freedom of living with God. The polished speakers at the pulpit and on the radio have little power to speak into a heart compared to the one who will simply take time to listen and understand.

You possess God's gifts. You may or may not know what they are. Tragically, some never discover them and die without ever realizing what joy is found in fulfilling these gifts by using them for His glory. This is the best and highest pleasure that this life offers: to serve God with the gifts He has given us. Knowing that you are working in the Master's will, with the tools he gave you gives a sense of fulfillment that words fail to describe. I want this for you.

Peer counseling may or may not be what God has for you in this life. But one sure way to learn this is to give it a try. Some have made attempts to counsel and quickly realized it does not fit who God made them to be. Others try it and soon find that they have been looking for this work all their lives. It brings out a part of them that has been dormant and awakens them to life closer to God Himself.

You may not be in a position to be part of a counseling ministry, but listening and connecting with people on deeper spiritual levels is always possible. Listening is the key. It is not what our prideful self initially wants to do, but it is what God wants us to do. We have great power when we listen. We can resolve personal conflicts, help others discover their gifts and purposes, and dissolve loneliness in others and ourselves, resulting in relationships that are supernatural. These deeper connections are more fulfilling and more of what God intended for us to have. This is all possible through selfless listening.

God is calling us to look outside of ourselves and connect with the hurting. Jesus did. In fact, they were his preferred associates and friends. We have the very words of life, and a Great Spirit to direct us. This is the answer for an ailing world. To withhold it is a serious offense to God.

I want to encourage you to act. God will put the first step in your heart. He will give it to you, and then you must take it. It might appear silly or awkward or it may be something you have never done before, but do not worry. God will walk with you. It is "Godfidence;" having faith that God is with you and is helping you to fulfill His purpose in your life. "Godfidence" will give you power in your spirit to do the hard things. You will be blessed by it and the world will be blessed by it. Reclaim your God-given work to care for the soul. It is God's only plan.

Notes

Chapter 1: Why This Book Is Needed

1. The following references are from theorists who looked at personal characteristics in general and identified those that might be ideal for the helping professional:

C.R. Rogers, *On Becoming a Person* (Boston: Houghton Mifflin, 1961).

A. Ivey, *Microcounseling: Innovations in Interviewing Training* (Springfield, IL: Charles C. Thomas,1971).

R.R. Carkhuff and C. Truax, "Lay Mental Health Counselors," *Journal of Consulting Psychology.* (Vol. 29, No. 5, 1969).

A. H. Maslow, *Toward a Psychology of Being,* Second Edition (NY: Van Nostrant Reinhold, 1968).

S. M. Jourard, *The Transparent Self: Revised Edition* (NY: Van Nostrand Reinhodt, 1971).

2. I do not have the citation of this study that I heard while in school in the late 1980's, but the work of William F. Brown is most likely the source of this discussion:

William F. Brown, "Effectiveness of Paraprofessionals: the Evidence," *Personnel and Guidance Journal.* (Vol. 53, No. 4, December 1974, p. 257-263).

Other articles that include summaries and discussion of peer counseling studies are:

Ruth H. Frisz, "Peer Counseling: Establishing a Network in Training and Supervision," *Journal of Counseling & Development.* (Vol. 64, No.7, March 1986, p. 457).

Judith A. Tindall, "Peer Counseling: An In-Depth Look at

Training Peer Helpers, " Third Edition (Muncie, IN: Accelerated Development Inc., 1989).

S. H. Scott and R. W. Warner, "Research in Counseling," *Personnel and Guidance Journal.* (Vol. 53, No. 3, November 1974, p. 228-231.)

3. A discussion of higher divorce rates among psychiatrists is found at : www.nationalreviewofmedicine.com/issue/2006/03_1 55/3_physians_life02_05.html

The suicide rate in helping professionals is well documented and is currently seen in research regarding physicians. Physicians have a suicide rate that is double the general population and psychiatrists have the highest rates among all physicians.

Rick, et al, "Suicides by Psychiatrists: A study of Medical Specialists," *Journal of Clinical Psychiatry.* (August 1980).

4. Benjamin Beit-Hallahmi, "Curiosity, Doubt, and Devotion: The Beliefs of Psychologists and the Psychology of Religion, " Article included in: H. Newton Malony, *Current Perspectives in the Psychology of Religion* (Grand Rapids, MI.: Wm. B. Eerdmans Publishing, 1979).

Chapter 3: The Danger From Within

1. Scott Simpson, "God's Love as God's Presence, 2010." Author's private collection.

Chapter 8: Miscellaneous Helpful Things

1. *The Power for True Success: How to Build Character in Your Life* (Oak Brook, IL: Institute in Basic Life Principles, 2001).

Chapter 12: Marriage Mentoring

1. *Prepare to Last* (Dallas, TX: Marriage Today).

Copyright 2006 by Life Innovations, Inc. Minneapolis MN.

preparetolast.com

2. *Marriage 911 First Response* (Branson, MO: National Institute of Marriage, 2007). nationalmarriage.com